A GUIDE TO THE IP

2020

All You Need to Know and a How -To Manual on Operating and Getting the Best from Your iPhone Second Generation

Bernard Gates

TABLE OF CONTENT

3

5

Introduction

The iPhone SE 2020 has one major aim: to launch a new iPhone for less coin than ever, and it does that creditably. For just $399 / £419 / AU$749 you can purchase a brand-new mobile phone from Apple. It ranks among the best iPhones ever created by Apple and it's now within your reach.

It's water resistant, but it does have some cons owing to the older design: it doesn't come with a headphone jack at the bottom

Apple may have kept the same old design as the iPhone 8 but the inside stuff has notably improved – particularly the new A13 Bionic chipset inside, which adds speed almost everywhere and actually improves the performance over the older 4.7-inch models.

The A13 bionic chipset has upped the camera performance too, despite no perceivable adjustment to the specs of the sensor since the iPhone 8. The iPhone SE camera is basically using the same set of lenses, and megapixel count, as the iPhone 8, with a 12MP camera, a six-element lens and a sapphire glass cover for strength. Apple also improved the quality of the images

The front-facing camera, a 7MP affair, has also been given smarter capabilities. The quality of the images is good – they're sharp and clean; In terms of video too, the overall power of the iPhone SE 2020 is as good as anything Apple is offering elsewhere in its lineup: you can shoot 4K video at up to 60 frames per second

Battery life is probably one of the biggest gripes with the iPhone SE 2020 – it's not going to see you through a day unless of course, you use it sparingly. The total charging speed is around one hour and 50 minutes for a full, dead-to-100% recharge, but the 5W charger that comes in the box will be a lot slower.

The iPhone SE price starts at $399 / £419 / AU$749 / Rs 42,500, meaning it's the same price in the US as the original iPhone SE (but higher in the UK). The base model comes with 64GB of storage, with 128GB and 256GB models also available for a higher price. The 128GB costs $449 / £469 / AU$829 while the 256GB costs $549 / £569 / AU$999.

Design and display: The iPhone SE has a similar design and display as the iPhone 8 from 2017. Apple has put its EarPods in the iPhone SE box, which use the phone's Lightning connector in place of the 3.5mm headphone jack. The display on the iPhone SE 2020 might not be immersive, but it will pass.

Now that we are done with the preliminaries, let's get to down to helping you navigate your way around your new device

Chapter 1: Setting up your new iPhone SE 2020

When you turn on your new iPhone for the first time, you'll be greeted with "Hello" in a variety of languages. It's basically the same even if you're starting from ground up, restoring from another iPhone, or switching from Android.

Moving Data and Stuff From A Previous Phone

Basically, you have three options to move data and settings from your old iPhone to a new iPhone. First, you can use the Quick Start feature which is the easiest one, restore from iTunes/Finder, and restore from iCloud. Just make sure you have backed up data of your old iPhone to iCloud or iTunes/Finder, just in case the Quick Start method fails. Be sure not to forget to update the software before you begin. For you to be able to use Quick Start, both devices have to run iOS 12 or later. Find below, the steps to set up iPhone SE using the Quick Start option:

- The first step is to make sure both iPhones are plugged to power sources and Wi-Fi.

- Next you turn on your brand-new iPhone SE and place it next to your previous iPhone.

- Once the Quick Start prompt appears on the old iPhone, click on **Continue**.

- Next, verify on your new iPhone SE if there is an animation coming on its display. If it's there, then place your old iPhone on the top of the new one to scan the animation.

- Next, you put in your passcode on the new iPhone, the one that you use to unlock your previous iPhone.

- Now, on your new device, follow the on-screen instruction to set up the Touch ID.

- When you get to the **Transfer Your Data** screen, tap **Transfer from iPhone** and let the process finish.

In case you don't have your old iPhone anymore, it's still possible for you to restore its contents to your new iPhone without stress. All you need do is follow the steps to set up iPhone SE from iCloud or iTunes/Finder back up.

- Power on your new iPhone SE by pressing and holding the power button on the top right of the phone until the Apple logo appears.

- Next, On the Quick Start screen, tap **Set Up Manually**.

- Next, select a Wi-Fi network and enter its password.

- Next, on the **Data & Privacy** screen, tap **Continue** after you read the statement.

- When you get to the next screen, tap **Continue** to set up Touch ID.

- Now, create a 6-digit passcode or tap **Passcode Options** at the bottom of the screen to choose the other password type options. Re-enter the passcode you choose on the next screen to confirm.

- Next, On the **Apps & Data** screen, select **Restore from iCloud Backup** or **Restore from iTunes Backup**.

- Enter the Apple ID of your previous iPhone and the password.

- Click **Agree** to confirm that you have read the Terms and Conditions.

- Click the latest backup on the screen and tap **Continue** on the following screen.

- The restoring process may take several minutes to complete.

How to Set Up iPhone SE As A New Phone

You can set up iPhone SE as a new phone. The basic requirements before starting the setup process are an Apple ID and its password and an Internet connection.

- Power on the phone by pressing and holding the power button on the top right of your iPhone SE and you will be greeted with a 'Hello' screen.

- Press the home button to continue the setup process.

- Select a language, then choose your country or region.

- On the Quick Start screen, select **Set up Manually**.

- Choose a WIFI network and enter the password. In case you have inserted a SIM card to your iPhone and have an active cellular data, select **Use Cellular Connection** at the bottom of the screen and select **Continue**.

- Next, follow the on-screen prompts to set up Touch ID. You are to set up Touch ID on both side thumbs, the right and left side.

- when you are done setting up Touch ID, choose **Set Up as New iPhone** on the **Apps & Data** screen. (more on the touch ID in a separate chapter)

- Now, enter your Apple ID and its password or select **Don't have an Apple ID or forgot it?** on the bottom of the screen. Next, follow the prompts to create a new Apple ID.
- When you get to the **Express Settings** screen, tap **Continue** or **Customize Settings**.
- Tap **Get Started** to start using your iPhone SE.
- You have the option to customize the settings and add some apps later on.

Moving Data From an Android Device

If you have been using an android device and made the decision to join the apple family, you will need to transfer all your stuff from the android phone to your new iPhone SE. The good news is that Apple has an app designed for new users making the switch from android to iOS. You can find it in the google play store. The first thing you need to do is to get the move to iOS on your android device. Note that you won't be able to transfer your android apps because they are not compatible with the Apple platform. You also won't be able to get your music and passwords moved too. Also keep in the mind that you can only transfer from an android device to a iPhone running iOS 9 or higher. All that being said, follow the guide below:

Set up your iPhone SE till you get to the display titled: "**Apps & Data**

Click on the "**move Data from Android**" option

- From your android device, access the **google play store** and search for **"move to iOS"**
- Next, open the **move to iOS** listing.
- Click **install.**
- **Agree** to the permissions request

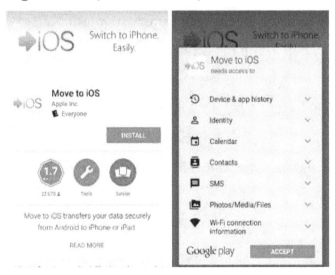

- **Open** after its installed.

- Click **continue** on both devices.

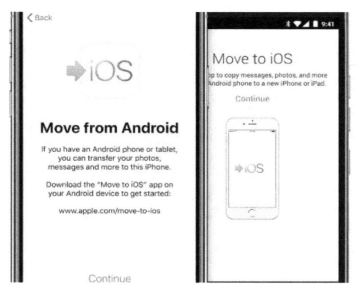

- Click **Agree** and then **Next** on your Android device

- From your **Android device,** key in the **12-digit** code shown on your iPhone SE.

- When you key in the code, the two devices will connect over a wi-fi connection and identify the data that can be moved in between both of them.

- You will be asked if you would like to move your google account information, chrome book marks, contacts, messages, photos and videos etc.

- Your android device will move the selected data to your new iPhone Once the data transfer is done, select continue setting up your iPhone and set up a new Apple ID or if you happen to already have an existing one, you can log in.

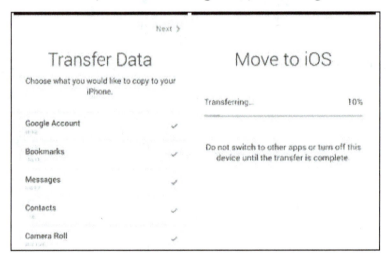

When you have completed the set-up process, you will be asked to log in to the accounts you just moved from your old Android device and that's it. You can begin to use your new device.

Moving Data To Your iPhone VIA iCloud

If you are inclined towards this option, then find below, the process you Can utilize to get it done:

- Go to **Settings** on your old device as shown above.

- Select the **Apple ID** banner

- Select **iCloud**

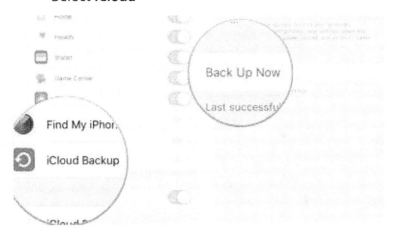

- Select **Back up now.**

- Power off your old device when the backup is done and take out the **sim card** from the old device especially if you are going to use it in the new iPhone.

- The backup must be completed before you move ahead to the next step.

- Next, you place the **sim** into the new device; that's if you want to use it in the new phone and power on the backed up new device.

- Push the home button and obey the prompts to select your preferred language and activate your wi-fi network.

- Next, you sign in to your **iCloud account.**

- Select **next** and then select **Agree**

- Repeat the above step (select agree) and Select the **backup** just completed.

You are done. Move on with setting up your new iPhone SE.

Transferring Your Data via the macOS Catalina Option

- Tether your old iPhone to your Mac computer which should be running macOS Catalina.

- Next, tap on the **finder** icon in the bar to get directed to a fresh finder window.

- Tap on your **iPhone** under the **locations** display

- You will next be asked to **trust** your iPhone.

- Next, you will click the **checkbox** for **Encrypt local Backup.**

- You will be required to Setup a **password** If this your first use of encrypted backups.

- Select **Backup now.**

- When you are done, disconnect your **old iPhone** and shut it down. If you intend to use the **sim** in your old device in the new one, take it out.

- When the backup is done, transfer the **sim** to the new **iPhone** and power it up.

- Once again, tether the **new iPhone** to the Mac.

- Push the home button on your **iPhone** and obey the set-up prompts.

- Next, click **Restore from Mac or PC** and Select your new iPhone from **locations** in the finder window and tap **Restore from this backup as shown:**

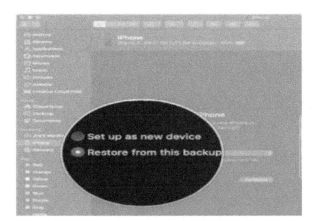

- Select your **recent backup** from the drop-down options and select **Continue.**

- Key in your **password** and tap **Restore** if you did an encrypted backup if you are interrogated by the finder.

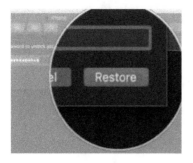

That's it. You all done. You can now move on with the remaining part of setting up your new iPhone SE.

Moving your data via macOS Mojave and older

- You have to have the latest version of **iTunes.**

- Connect your **old iPhone** to your **mac system.**

- Open **iTunes.**

- Tap on the iPhone icon in the **menu** bar

- Select **Encrypt backup.** You may be required to set-up a **password** if it's your first time encrypting a backup.

- Next, select **Backup now**.

- Disregard **Backup apps** if it comes up.

- Disconnect your **old device** when the **backup** process is complete.

- Remove your **sim** from the **old iPhone** if you plan to reuse it in the **new iPhone** and then wait for the **backup** process to run.

- When you are ready to resume, equip the new iPhone with the sim (either previous used or new sim).

- Switch on the new device and connect it to your Mac. Obey the set-up directions till you activate your wi-fi.

- Click **Restore from iTunes** backup.

- From your Mac or windows PC, opt for **Restore from this backup.**

- Select the most **recent backup** from the options.

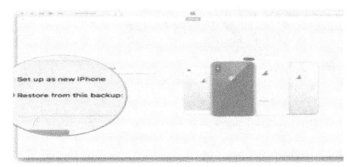

- Select **Continue**.

- Finally, in case you are prompted, key in your **password** if the backup was encrypted.

At this point, you have to keep your new device connected to iTunes till the transfer is executed which in some cases, may take a little bit of time based on the amount of data being moved.

Chapter 2: The Touch ID

The touch ID is a security feature designed by Apple to allow users of the iPhone SE enjoy the advantage of an alpha numeric password to access or make use of their phone via their fingerprint. Using Touch ID to open or access your device is as easy as placing any of the registered fingerprints on the home button. So, let's look at the steps to set-up this feature.

Setting up the touch ID on the iPhone SE

To set up the touch ID function, you would have begun the process of the initial set-up of a new or restored iPhone and gotten to the point where you would be asked to choose either to set-up the touch ID immediately or later. So, either way or option, the process runs as below:

- Open the **Settings** app from the home screen display.

- Click on **Touch ID & Passcode**

- Enter your passcode for authentication if interrogated. You would be required to set one up if you didn't do so when you were setting up your new device.

- Next, click on the **Add a fingerprint** button

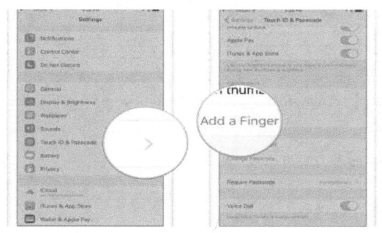

- Place the finger chosen on the **home button** and hold it there until you get a buzz. Repeat severally until **Touch ID** informs you that the first step is done and it now needs peripheral data.

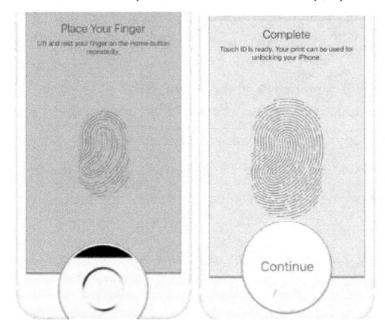

- Next, place the edges of the same finger you are registering on the **home button** and hold it there until you get the same buzz. Repeat same process with a different edge until have registered the whole surface of the finger.

- Click on **Continue** to complete the process as shown above

As pointed out above, you can still register up to 4 additional fingers cutting across family, friends and colleagues. The process is basically the same. Remember that you do not have to divulge your password to include other fingers in the data base.

Identifying a Touch ID Fingerprint

- Open the **Settings** app

- Click open the **Touch ID & Passcode.**

- Key in your **passcode** when required.

- Press your **registered fingerprint** on the **home button.**

- Keep an eye out for the display that alternates between white and gray. It would enable you to accurately tag the different fingerprints.

Tagging a Touch ID fingerprint.
Pursuant to item 7 above, here's a detailed guide to knowing which fingerprint is which. You can tag them to make easier to find the particular one you seek. Just follow the guide below:

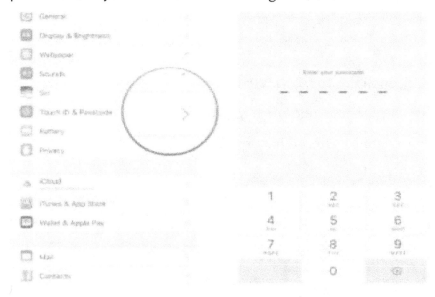

- First, access the **Settings** app
- Next, click on **Touch ID & Passcode**.
- Key in your **passcode** when required.
- Click on the desired **finger** that you wish to rename.
- Enter a new, if possible, more customized name for the finger print and then click the **Done** button.

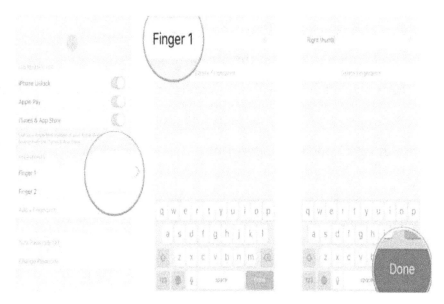

You are to do this same procedure outlined above for all the other fingerprints till you can easily and positively identify them all.

Turning off Touch ID

Touch ID is supposed to take some stress off you but if you prefer not to use it for some features like the lock screen, Apple pay, iTunes and App stores, it's possible to do just that by following the steps below:

- Go to **settings**.

- Click the **Touch ID & Passcode button**.

- Input your **passcode** at the prompt

- Turn off Touch ID for the functions you don't want. E.g. iPhone unlock, Apple Pay, iTunes and App store.

Deleting a Touch ID fingerprint

- Open the **Settings app**.

- Click on **Touch ID & Passcode.**

- Key in your **passcode** when required.

- Next, click on the particular **fingerprint** you want to remove.

- Click on **delete fingerprint** and then click **done** at the bottom.

In case you want to expel more than one fingerprint, just re-do 4-6 from the steps itemized above.

Using Touch ID For Purchases.

Asides your Apple ID, you can decide to use your Touch ID to pay for purchases from the Apple store. To do this, follow the guide below:

- Ensure that the App store and iTunes are activated.

- Open **Settings** and tap on **Touch ID & Passcode.**

- Next, verify that the switch for **iTunes** and the **App store** are in the on position. If they are not, activate them as shown below:

When you have done this, if you desire to make any purchase from the iTunes or App store, just open the desired one, tap the item you want to purchase and you will get the **Touch ID** icon at the bottom of the screen. To pay is as simple as pressing the home button.

Using Touch ID To Lock the Notes Function Of Your iPhone SE.

For users that have important or sensitive information that they would like to secure from prying eyes, you can use Touch ID as a guard to protect such information through the following steps:

- Open notes from the home screen.

- Click on a **note** you have or type a **new one.**

- Next, click on the **share** button and then click **lock note.**

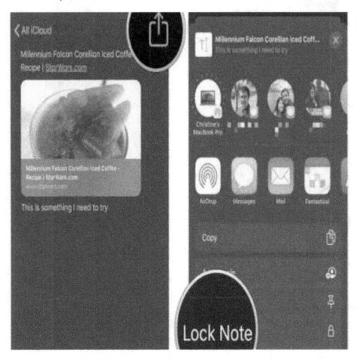

- Key in a **password** and **verify** again when prompted.

- You may have to include a **hint** for the chosen **password.**

- Turn on **Touch ID.**

- Click on **Done** to confirm that you want the note locked.

Chapter 3: Setting up "Hey Siri"

During the initial setting up process of your new device, you will be asked if you would like to use the "Hey Siri" voice activation option. If you elect to activate it later, find below, the process of doing so:

- Open **Settings** from your home screen

- Click on **Siri & Search**

- Select the **"listen for 'Hey siri"** button to turn it on.

You will need to train the technology to recognize your voice.

- Click on **continue** on the set up **"Hey Siri"** page

- Next, say **"Hey Siri"** using your voice

- Say again **"Hey siri send a message"**

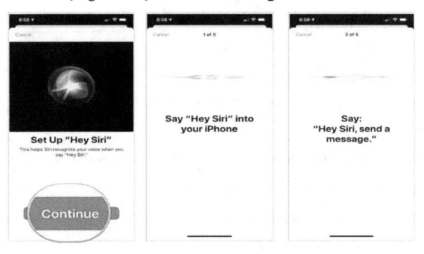

- To get further used to the technology and for the virtual assistant to register your voice, from the screen display, you will be prompted to make some statements like:

'"hey siri, How's the weather today?"

"hey siri, set a timer for three minutes"

"Hey siri, play some music"

- Finally, click **done** on the "Hey siri" is ready display.

Say:	Say:	And finally, say:
"Hey Siri, how's the weather today?"	"Hey Siri, set a timer for three minutes."	"Hey Siri, play some music."

If you get it done properly, then siri would have registered your voice and is now at your service.

Using "Hey siri"

- Make sure you are situated within proper audio range of your device.
- Next, speak loudly for your device to pick up:" **Hey siri"**
- Let **"Hey siri"** know the task you want it to carry out. For e.g., set an alarm for 5am, call Jason on speaker, etc.

Chapter 4: Setting up Apple ID

The Apple ID is an Apple account that allows you to purchase stuff or items from the apple store like books, movies, Apps, games, movies, and music from iTunes, sync your contacts, reminders, and calendars through iCloud and use iMessage and Facetime in the messages apps. If you already have an apple ID, then you only need sign in with your apple ID but if this is your first apple device, you need to create one. Find how to go about it below:

Creating an Apple ID

- Go to the **Setting**s app.

- On the top of the screen, click on **Sign in to your iPhone**.

- Tap on **Don't have an Apple ID or forgot it?**

- On the following screen, choose **Create Apple ID**

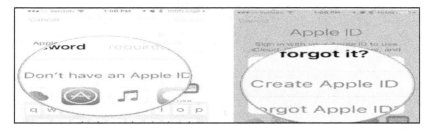

- Next, key in your date of birth and click on **Next**.

- Enter your name: first and last and click on **Next**.

- Select to **sign up with a current email address** or if you would prefer to **get a free iCloud email address**.

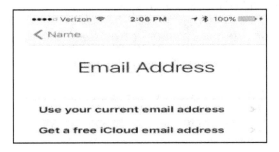

- enter your email address and create your chosen **password**.

- Repeat the **password**.

- Next, you are to select three security questions and enter the answers to the chosen questions and click on next.

- Next, **Agree** to the Terms and Conditions.

- You can decide to Merge or not to merge, to sync iCloud data from calendars, contacts, Safari, and reminders.

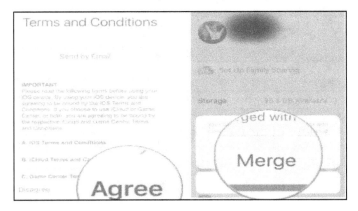

- Select **Ok** to agree that you want the **Find My** enabled.

Signing In to iCloud With an Existing Apple ID

- Go to the **Settings** app.

- Next, on top of the screen, click on **Sign in to your iPhone.**

- Enter your login details and click **Sign In.**

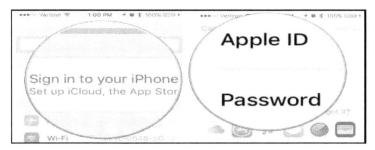

- Enter your **password** when required

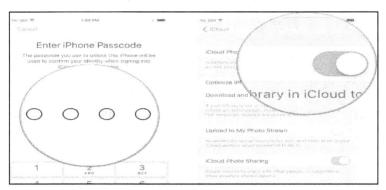

- Activate or deactivate the option for Apps using iCloud, based on your preferred settings.

Signing Out of iCloud

- From the **Settings** app, go to the top of the screen and select your **Apple ID**.

- Scroll to the bottom of the screen and click on **Sign Out.**

- Enter your Apple ID password for this account and select **Turn Off.**

- Turn on the buttons for all the data you want to retain on your iPhone.

- From the top right side of the screen, click **Sign Out.**

- Click again on **Sign Out** to affirm what you have just done.

Chapter 5: Setting up Apple Pay

With Apple pay, it's possible for users to purchase items either online or in-store. All it would entail is just a touch of the Home button and a scan of your fingerprint; But before you can start using it, you have to set it up first. Here's how:

The first step is to add a card to Apple pay.

- Open the **walle**t app from the home screen display.

- Click on the **+button** on the top right side of the screen

- Click on **Continue** or **Next** on the Apple pay screen

- Next, you have 2 options for entering the details of your credit or debit card. Either you **manually** input them or you **scan with the**

phone camera. (should you decide to go with the camera scan option, make sure that the credit or debit card has embossed numbers because, the photo detection system does not register flat numbers)

- Click **Next** on the card details display screen.

- Input the **expiration date** and **security code** of the card manually.

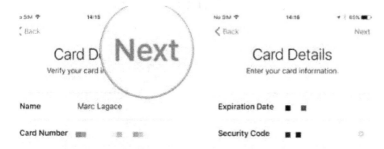

- Click **Next**

- Click **Agree** to accept the terms and conditions

- Click **Agree** again.

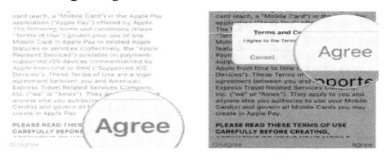

- Select **Next** after you choose verification method and tap **Enter code.**

- Key in the verification code that was given you. This could either be a text, call or email based on your chosen verification method.

- Click on **Next** and then click on **Done.**

Card Verification

Enter Your American Express Verification Code.

Card Activated

"Corporate Platinum Card®" is ready for Apple Pay.

Follow this same procedure in case you ever wish to add more debit or credit cards.

Changing the Initial Card for Apple Pay

The apple pay system allows you to register and effect payment for purchases and transactions using several credit and debit cards. You can seamlessly switch between them to make payments.

- Go to the **Settings** app on your device

- Open **Wallet & Apple pay**

- Click on **Default card**

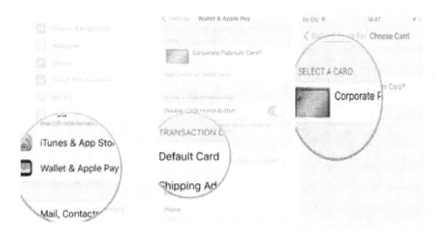

- Select the card you would prefer to use as the standard for making purchases and transactions.

Removing a Card from Apple Pay
- Go to **Settings**
- Click on **wallet & Apple pay**

- Click on the **card** you would like to remove
- Finally, click on **Remove this card**

Chapter 6: Setting up and using the haptic touch

The haptic touch is a new way to perform and get your device to carry out tasks. It simply involves long pressing to activate actions. It lets you do more effortlessly.

Rearranging or deleting Apps on the Home screen with Haptic touch

- Long press on the home screen icon you want to open quick for

- Now click on task you want to execute

Widgets

- For widgets, long press on the home screen icon you want to call up widgets for.

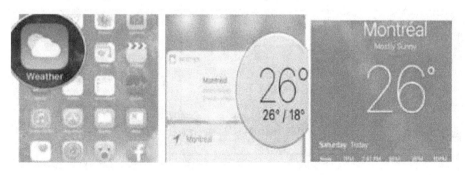

- Click on the **widget** to go to access the tap.

In case you are downloading apps, there are steps you can take to give priority to one specific App over the others and canceling the ones you no longer need.

- **Long press** on the installation icon you want to open quick actions

 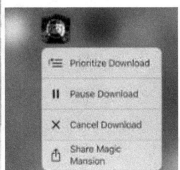

- Next, click on the action you want to perform
- Click on the action you want to execute

Using Haptic Touch with Notifications
- Long press on a **Notification**

- Click on the **notification** and click on the **X button** to dismiss the notification

With Haptic touch, you can wipe the notification center

- Long press on the **x button** above your notifications

- Click on **clear all notifications**

Customizing the Haptic Touch

- Open **Settings** from your home screen

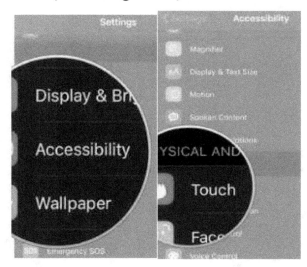

- Click on **Accessibility**

- Click on **Touch**

- Click on **Haptic touch** and select either **fast** or **slow** to change the time it takes to set off the Haptic touch.

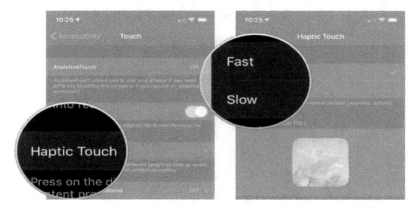

Chapter 7: Setting Up and Using the Control Center

The control center gives the user easy and quick access on their device to quite a number of functions and features. It's possible for owners to execute actions right from the control center. Here's how:

- Open **Settings**
- Click on **Touch ID & Passcode**
- Key in your **passcode** when required
- Navigate down and activate the **control center** button

How to Open the Control Center on Your Device
- From the bottom edge of the screen, swipe up towards the top of the screen

Customizing the Control Center

The control center allows the user the ability to choose the functions that can be accessed via the control center.

Adding Controls to the Control Center
The first step is to make sure that you have the control center feature or function enabled on your device.

- Go to the **Settings** App

- Click **control center**

- Click on **Customize Controls**
- Click the **add button (+)** next to a control under the more controls display

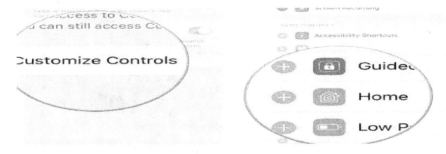

Organizing the Hierarchy of Controls in the Control Center

In case a user wants to organize the control center in such a way that the more frequently used functions are easily and readily accessed while the less used ones are placed at a lower position, here are the steps to follow:

- Go to the **Settings App** and click on **Control Center**
- Press and hold a **control** till it goes into hover mode
- Next, drag the **control** to its new place on the list

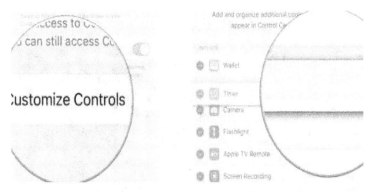

You can play around with the control center till it fits your desired setting and appearance.

Removing Controls from the Control Center

- Open the **settings App** and click **control center**

- Click **customize controls**

- Click the **remove button** which looks like this **(-)**. It's usually next to a control under the include section.

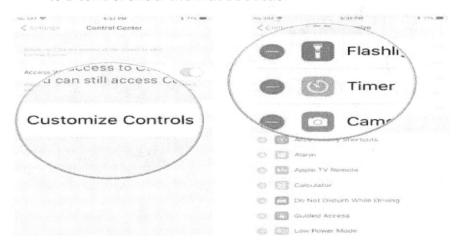

Disabling Control Center on the Lock Screen

- Open the **settings** App

- Click the **Touch ID & Passcode**

- Key in your **Passcode**

- Navigate down and deactivate the **Control Center** button

 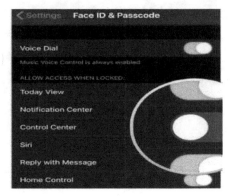

Disabling the Control Center from Apps

- Go to **Settings** and click **Control Center**

- Deactivate the **Access within Apps** button

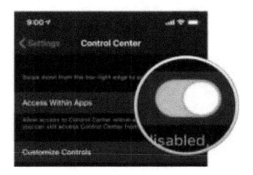

Chapter 8: Adjusting the default iPhone SE settings

Making Text Bolder and Bigger

- Open **Settings** and click **Accessibility**

- Click **Display and Text size**

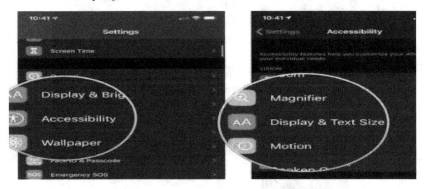

- Click **Larger Text**

- Click, hold and then drag the **slider** to change the text size

- In case you need the text to be even larger, click the button next to **Larger Accessibility Sizes**

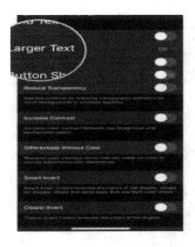

Changing the Text Buttons

- Open **Settings** and click **Accessibility**

- Click **Display and Text size**

- Next, tap the button next to **button shapes**

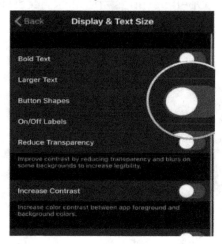

Reducing the White Point

- Launch **Settings** and **click Accessibility**

- Click **Display & Text size**

- Click the button next to **reduce white point**

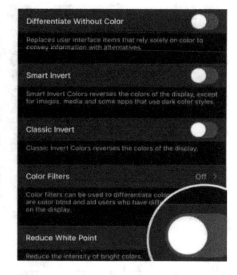

Deactivating Parallax and App Zooms

- Open **Settings** and click **Accessibility**

- Click **Motion**

- Activate the **button** next to **reduce motion** to the green "on" setting to activate **reduced motion**

 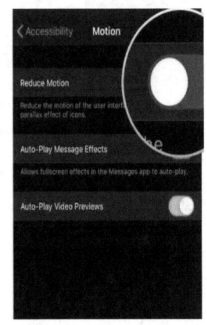

Turning off the Lower-case Keyboard

- Open **Settings** and go to **Accessibility**

- Click **Keyboards** under **Physical and motor**

- Click the **button** next to **Show lowercase keys** to turn it to the gray/black "off" position

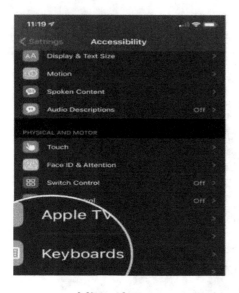 

Enabling Character Preview

- Open **Settings**

- Go to **General**

- Next, click on **Keyboard**

- Click the **button** next to **Character preview**

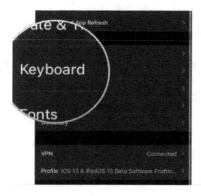 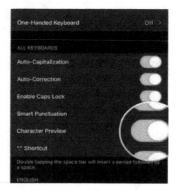

Turning off Reachability

This feature allows you to call down the top of the screen so you can have access to it via your thumb but if you find that you don't not actually need it, here's how to deactivate it:

- From **Settings** on your home screen, tap **Accessibility**
- Click **Touch**
- Click the **button** next to **Reachability** so it will be in the gray/black off position

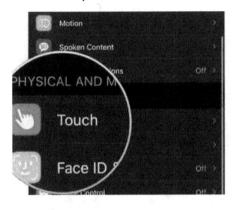 

Disabling" Shake to undo"

- Open **settings** and go to **Accessibility**
- Click **Touch**
- Click the **button** next to **Shake to undo** to deactivate it

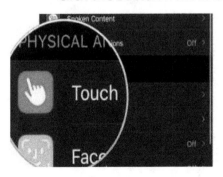 

Adjusting the Audio and Information Settings

To turn off lock sounds and keyboard clicks:

- Open **Settings**

- Click on **Sounds & Haptics**

- Navigate down and click on the **buttons** next to **Keyboard clicks** and **Lock sound** to activate or deactivate them

Adjusting the Maps Navigation Volume

- Open **Settings**

- Go to **Maps**

- Click **driving and navigation**

- Choose an option under **Navigation Voice Volume**

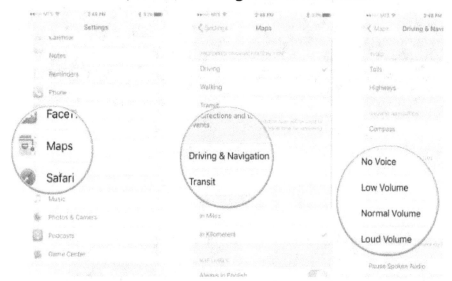

Siri Settings

Turning off Siri's voice:

- Open **Settings**

- Click **on Siri & Search**

- Deactivate the **button** for **Listen for "Hey Siri"**

Controlling Siri's Voice Feedback

- Open **Settings**

- Click on **Siri & Search**

- Click on **Voice Feedback**

- Choose from **Always on, Control with Ring switch** or **Handsfree only**

Deactivating Siri Suggestions

- From your screen, **swipe right** to get to Today view

- Next, **swipe up** to navigate down and click the **Edit** button at the bottom

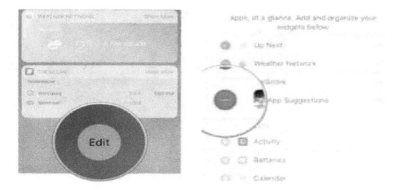

- Click the red circle with the **minus** in the center next to **siri App suggestions**

  - Next, click **remove**

Routing Calls Manually to Speaker or Bluetooth

- Open **Settings** and Click **Accessibility**

- Tap **Touch**

- Navigate down and click **Call Audio Routing**

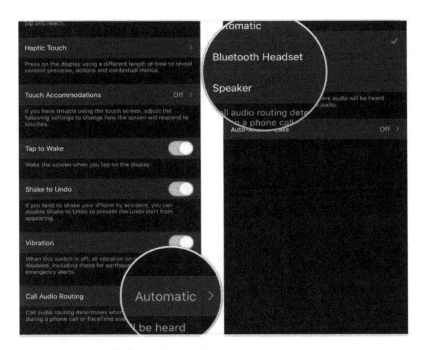

- Click **Bluetooth headset** or **Speaker**

Chapter 9: Taking a screen shot with your iPhone

This is a handy feature for capturing images you ordinarily won't be able to get via normal means of photography or image capturing. It allows you to record virtually anything you can see on your screen.

How to take a Screen Shot:

- Get to the screen that has the **image or App** you want to capture.

- Set it the exact way you desire the shot to be or look like

- Push the **side button and home button** simultaneously as shown below

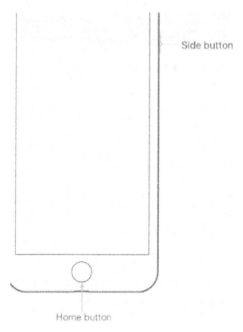

Side button

Home button

Viewing and Editing Screen Shots

- Launch the **photos** folder or App

- Click on **Albums**

- Click on **Screenshots**

- Select **Edit**

Taking a Screen Shot Using the Assistive Touch Capability of the iPhone SE

For users who may not be happy or comfortable with having to push two different buttons simultaneously to take a screen shot, it's possible to take a screen shot using just one simply to press button. Here's how:

- Go to **Settings**

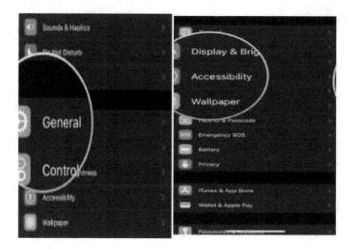

- Go to **General**

- Select **Accessibility**

- Enable the **Assistive touch** button (you will see a semi-transparent button added to the screen)

- Click on the **Customize top Level Menu**

- Next, click on the custom icon (with one star) and select **Screen shot** from the list

- To take a screenshot with the **Assistive touch,** click on the **Assistive button** and then tap the **screen shot** button.

You can replace the screen shot button with any of the default icons at any time you wish.

Chapter 10: Sim settings and operation

The SE is a dual-SIM iPhone that supports one nano-SIM and an eSIM. An eSIM is a digital SIM that will enable you to set up a cellular plan without a physical nano-SIM. With iOS 13, the two phone numbers can receive and make FaceTime and Voice calls as well as receive and send messages using iMessage, MMS, and SMS. You equally need to make sure that your service provider supports eSIM. Also, you will be not be able to use two SIMs from two different service providers if using a locked iPhone.

Setting Up Your Cellular Plan with an eSIM

The physical nano-SIM by default, is used for a cellular plan while the eSIM is used for other mobile plans but an eSIM can also serve as your only cellular plan if your service provider supports it. This eSIM is implanted digitally on your smartphone. You have several options to activate a cellular plan on an eSIM: you can use your carrier's iPhone app, scan a QR code provided by your supplier, or enter the information manually.

To Scan a QR Code

Use the steps below to activate your cellular plan:

- Go to the **Settings** app on your phone.
- select **Cellular.**
- Select **Add Cellular Plan.**
- Next, use your phone camera to scan the QR code given by the carrier. If asked for a confirmation code to activate the eSIM, key in the number provided by your carrier.

Using a service provider App

From the App Store, download the app for your service provider.

- Install the app.

- Next, buy a plan from the app.

- The app will pick the eSIM support on your iPhone.

- obey the guide on your screen to create a new plan.

Entering eSIM Information Manually

Follow the steps below to enter your plan manually:

- from **Settings,**

- select **Cellular.**

- Next, click on **Add Cellular Plan.**

- From the bottom of your screen, select **Enter Details Manually.**

- Next, key in the eSIM details, for e.g the phone number provided by your service provider.

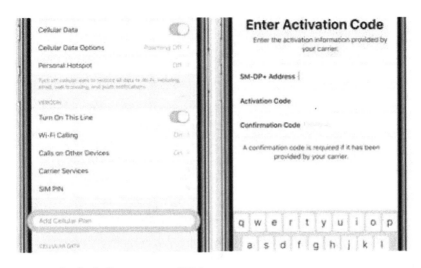

Switch Between eSIMs

It's possible for You to have more than one eSIMs on your phone but you are only allowed the use of one at any given point in time. To switch between eSIMs, find the steps below:

- launch **Settings.**
- select **Cellular.**
- select your preferred eSIM.
- Next, select **Turn on This Line.**

Erasing an eSIM

- from **Settings,** select **Cellular.**

- select the plan you want to delete.

- Click on **Remove Cellular Plan.**

Labelling Your Plans

- launch **Settings.** Select **Cellular.**

- Select the number you want to label.

- Next, click on **Cellular Plan Label** and choose from one of the default labels, or create a personal label.

- Tap **Done** on your keyboard when you are through.

Setting Your Default Number

- launch **Settings.** Select **Cellular.** Select **Default Line.**

- Choose your preference from the options on your screen.

- **Use (Plan Label) as your default line:** any plan label you choose from here will be used for data, SMS, and voice

- **Use (Plan Label) for cellular only:** this plan is designed for people traveling internationally, who want to use the line for data alone.

Let Your Phone Remember the Number to Use

To designate the number to use whenever you are calling a contact, do the following:

- Go to the Contacts app and search for the contact.

- Select the contact.

- Click on **Edit** at the top of your screen. Select **Preferred Line.**

- Next, click on the number you want to use for that contact.

- Choose the Number to Use for Call

  You can Switch Phone Numbers Before Making a Call with the Steps Below:

- To call the contacts in your Favorite list,

launch the Phone app and select the Favorite tab.

- click (i) beside the contact you want to call

- Tap on the current phone number showing on your screen

- Next, click on your second number to call with the other number

- If using the keypad to dial the number

- Key in the recipient's phone number

- Click on the label at the top of the screen

- Then choose the number you want to use.

- Choose Number to Use for a Message

Follow the Steps Below to Choose a Particular Phone Number to Send a Message With:

- Launch the Messages app.

- Click on the **New** button at the top right side of your screen.

- Enter the name of the recipient.

- Click on the label of the current phone number.

- Next, select your preferred number for messaging that contact.

Choosing the Number for Cellular Data

Follow the steps below to assign a number to use for cellular data:

- launch the Settings app.

- Click on **Cellular.**

- Click on **Cellular Data.**

- Then select your preferred number for cellular data.

Allow Cellular Data Switching

Activate **Allow Cellular Data Switching** so that if you are on a voice call on a voice-only phone number, that number will automatically switch to both Voice and Data.

- launch the Settings app.
- Select **Cellular.**
- Click on **Cellular Data.**
- switch on **Allow Cellular Data Switching**

Manage Cellular Settings

Follow the steps below to change the cellular settings for each of your plans:

- Open the **Settings** app. Click on **Cellular.**
- select the number you want to change.
- Then select each option and set to your preference.

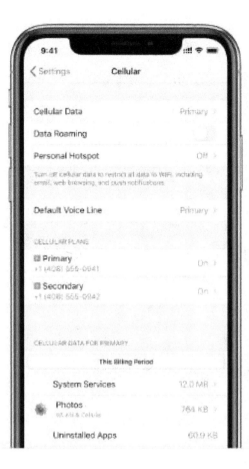

Chapter 11: iMessaging

It's an instant messaging service that connects Apple users through iPhone, iPad, Mac or Apple watch. Users can send text, picture, video, sound and location.

Before you can start enjoying these features, you need to set up first. Here's how:

If you have enabled iCloud on your iPhone, it's possible that the iMessaging function was activated automatically but if not, follow these steps below:

- Open **Settings**

- Click **Messages**

- Click on the iMessage **On/Off switch.**

Turning on "Read receipts" on or off in iMessages.

This function is basically used to allow your contacts see if you have seen their iMessages

- Open **Settings**

- Click on **Messages**

- Click on the **Send Read Receipts on/off** switch.

Turning Messages Previews on/off

- Open **Settings**

- Click **Notifications**

- Click **Messages**

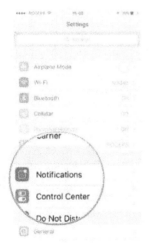

- Click **show previews**

- Next, click on the option you prefer

Telling the Difference Between Sending an iMessage or an SMS/MMS

iMessages are contained in a blue bubble and usually work if you are on wi-fi or on cellular data. It works between Apple devices.

SMS/MMS are contained in a green bubble and work with cellular network. It works when messages are sent to other devices that are not Apple devices.

Sending a Text Message via iMessage

- Open **Messages**
- Click **Compose** in the upper right corner of the display screen
- Next, enter the name of the **Recipient**

- Tap out your message in the **message bar or field**

- Click on the **Send** arrow next to the message

Sending a New Photo or Video using Messages

- Open **Messages** and click on the **conversation** in which you would like to send a picture

- Click on the **camera** button to the left of the text field

- Click the **shutter button.** You can also swipe right to take a video and wait for a second or two and a new screen will appear.

- You can now **edit** the photo before sending it by tapping the blue **send button** in the right corner at the bottom of the screen.

Sending an Existing Photo or Video via iMessage

- Open **Messages**

- Click on the **conversation** in which you want to send a photo

- Click on the **Apps button** to the left of the text field

- Tap **the Photo Apps button**

- Click the **photo or video** you would like to send

- If you desire, you can add a **comment** and then click on the **blue** send button

Sending your Current Location Using iMessage

If you want to send someone your current location without having to constantly share your location, here's how you can do it:

- Click on the **name** at the top of the conversation screen in a messages conversation
- Next, click on the **info** button that appears below the name
- Click on **Send My Current Location**

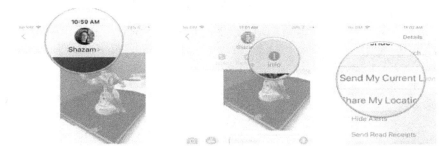

Sharing your Location for a Period of Time

- Open **Messages**
- Click on the chosen **conversation**
- Click on the **name** at the top of the **conversation** screen

- Next, click on the **info** button that appears below the name

- Select **Share My Location**

- Choose the **Duration** for which you would like to share your location

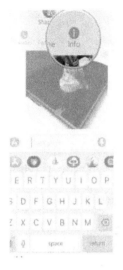

Sharing a Contact Card through iMessages Via the Contacts App

- Open the **Contacts** or **Phone** app

- Locate and click on the **contacts** you would like to share

- Next, tap on **Share Contact** close to the bottom of the screen

- Click on **Messages** and enter the name of **the Recipient**

- Click on **Send**

Sending your Location from the Maps

- Open the **Maps** app

- Locate the location you would like to share. If it's your current, click on the **location arrow** in order find yourself

- Swipe **up** from the screen bottom

- Next, tap the **Share** button

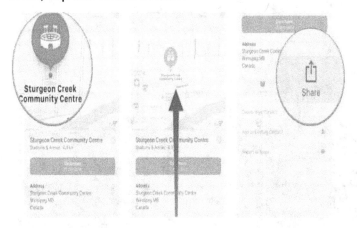

- Click on **Message**

- Enter the **name** of the person that you want to share your location with

- Next, click on **Send**

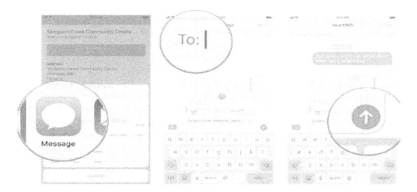

Sending Messages via iMessage using Siri

- Push and hold the **home button** to launch Siri

- Tell Siri that you want to **send a message,** giving details of the recipient e.g. name, phone number, iMessage linked email address.

- Dictate the **message.**

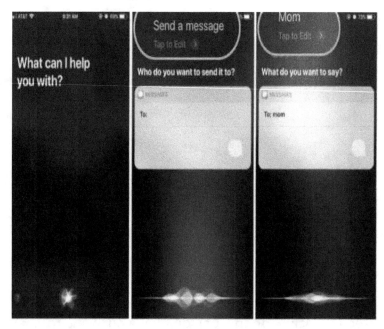

Wait for Siri to **confirm** the content of the dictated text

You can either say or click **Send**

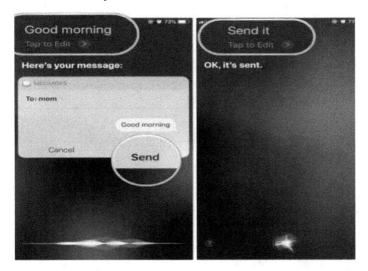

Changing Which Apple ID iMessage Uses on iPhone

Sometimes, it's possible for other people -maybe family members to view messages or content meant for your eyes and it can also go the other way round. This happens because the devices are using the same Apple ID. Here's how to fix this:

The first step is for all those involved to create and have their own unique iCloud account. When this has been done, do the following

- Go to **Settings.** Click **Messages.** Select **Send & receive**

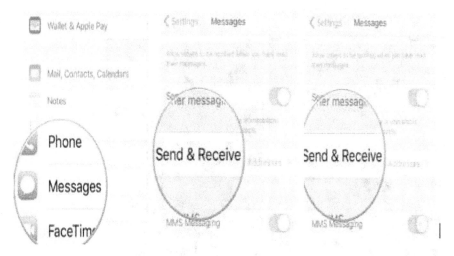

- Click the **Apple ID** at the top of the screen

- Click on **Sign out**

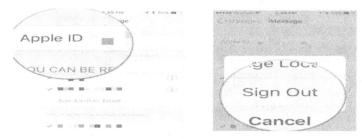

- Select **use your Apple ID for iMessage**

- Use your **Apple ID and password** to log in

- Click **sign in**

Chapter 12: Photos

The photos file of your phone is very handy for storing all the pictures and videos you take or make with your device. you can use the app for a variety of functions such as organizing, sharing and even editing videos or pictures through social media. Here's how to navigate through this very useful tool:

Creating a New Album in the Photos App

- Launch **Photos**

- Click **Albums**

- Click the **+ button** at upper left

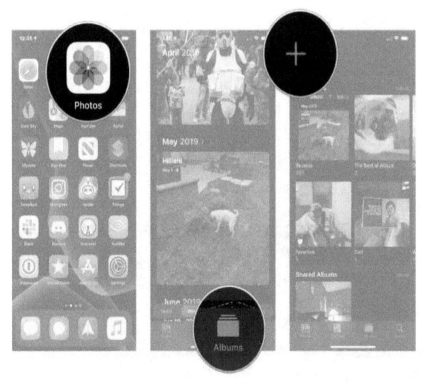

- Click **New Album**

- Give the **Album** a name

- **Save**

- Select the **photos** you want to include in the Album

- Click **Done**

Creating Shared Albums in the Photos App

- Launch **Photos**

- Click **Albums**

- Click **"+"** at upper left corner

- Click **New Shared Album**

- Give it a **name**

- Click **Next**

- Type out the **names** of the album recipients

- Click **Create**

- Click the **Shared Album**

 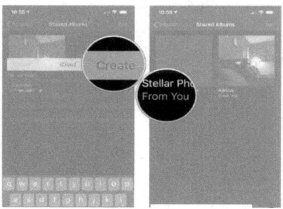

- Click the **+ button**

- Select the **photos** you want to add to the album

- Click **Done**

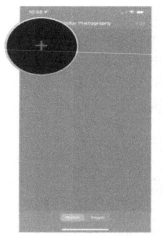  

Adding Photos and Videos to Existing Albums in the Photo App

- Launch **Photos**

- Click the **Photos** icon

- Click on either **Days** or **All Photos**

- Click **Select**

- Select the **photos** you would like to add to the album

- Click the **Share** button

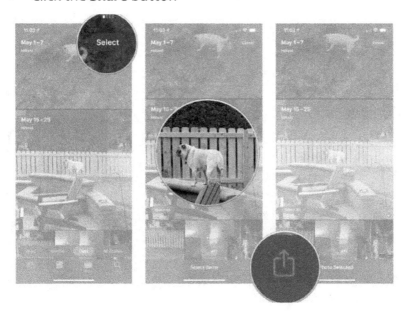

- Select either **Add to Album** or **Add to Shared Album**

- Click on the **Album** that you want to add the photos to

 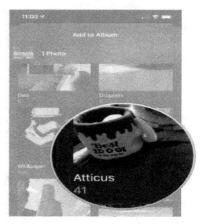

Navigating Between Moments, Collections and Years Smart Groups

- Open **Photos and** click the **back button** to top left of screen. To increase your search scope to days, months and years, just keep going back
- Click on a **photo or video thumbnail** to move to a smaller group

Moving Between Years, Months and Days

- Open **Photos**
- Click on the **Photos** icon

- Next, click on your desired timeline view: **Years, Months**, **Days** or **All photos**

If you want to back out of any view you are in, just click on the years, months or Days in the menu bar above the tabs for photos

Viewing Picture and Video Locations on a Map

- Open the **Photos** app and click on the **name** of the location above the group of photos which you want a location for

- Swipe upwards to find the **map.** The scrolling might take a little bit of time. Be sure that that you have location services activated beforehand otherwise, you won't be able to view the location of the photos

Viewing Picture and Video Locations on a Map in iOS 13

- Open **Photos**

- Navigate to the photos tab where you can select between **Years**, **Months** and **Days** and **All photos**

- Next, from the **Months** or **Days** view, click on the **"..."** button on the collection thumbnail

- Click **Show Map** and you will get to see the location where the photos were taken and this is dependent on if location services was enabled at the time of taking the pictures.

Quickly Locating a Photo or Video in Collections or Years

To cut through the probably hundreds if not thousands of images, especially due to the thumbnails that are so small to see, there's a scrubbing motion that enables you to quickly find what you seek:

- Open **Photos**

- Click on and hold the **Year or Collection view**

- Touch lightly and move your **finger** back and forth across the **collection.** You will be able to see a larger thumbnail view of each photo

- Next, press firmly on the **photo** you would like to see

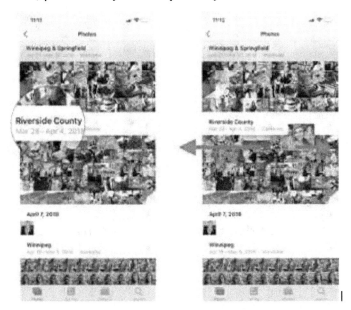

Quickly selecting a Month to Jump to from the Years View

- Open **Photos**

- Verify you are in the photos tab that organizes by **Years, Months and Days and** Click on the **Years** view in **Photos**

- Locate the **year** you would like to view

- **Drag** your finger horizontally across the tile

- Click on **collection tile** to jump into the month you left it on while scrubbing

Copying a Video or Picture to the Clipboard in Moments or Albums

- Open the **Photos** app

- Click **Select** to the top right of the screen

- Click the **video** or **photo** you would like to copy

- Click the share button to the bottom left of the screen

- Click copy on the popup menu

Quickly Copying Pictures or Videos from Moments to the Clipboard in iOS 13

- Open **Photos**

- Go to the **Photos** tab

- Locate the **photos** or **videos** you desire to share from the **All Photos** view

- Click **Select** to top right

- Select the **photos** or **videos** you want to share or **drag** your finger across rows and columns to quickly select a **batch**

- Click on **Share**

- Navigate down and select **Copy Photos**

Hiding Images
- Open the **Photos** app

- From the **Days, All photos** or default **Albums** view, click on the **Select** button

- Select the **photos** you want to hide. It's also possible to hide individual or stand-alone pictures as it is to equally hide a large batch

 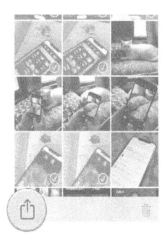

- Navigate down in the **share sheet**

- **Click on Hide**

- Next, **Confirm** that you want to hide the photos or click **Cancel** if you don't want to hide them anymore

  How to Unhide Photos
- Launch the **Photo** app

- Click on **Albums**

- Click on **Hidden Album**

- Click **Select** in the upper corner

- Select the **photo**s you want to unhide

- From the bottom row of share icons, click **Unhide**

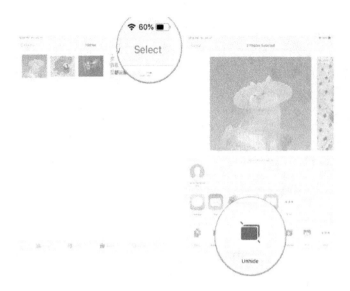

Unhiding Photos or Albums in iOS 13

- Go to **Photos**

- Click **Albums**

- Navigate to the bottom where you will see other **Albums**

- Click **Hidden**

- Click **Select**

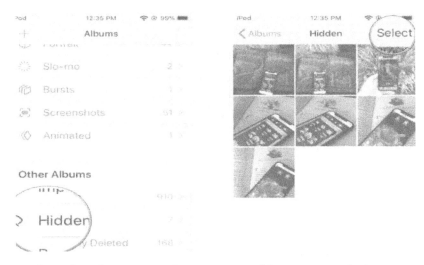

- Select the photos or videos you would want to unhide

- Navigate down and click **Unhide**

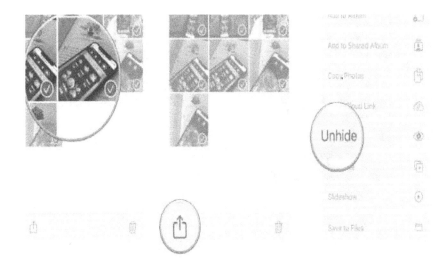

Locating Memories in Photos

- Open the **Photos** app

- Click **Memories** in the menu bar at screen bottom

- Click on a **memory** to view it

Searching Memories

- Open **Photos**

- Click on **Search** tab

Type the **search terms** you seek to help find a particular memory

Starting a Slide Show from Memories

- Go to **photos**

- Click on the **For You** tab

- Navigate to the **Memories** section and click **See All**

- Choose a **memory** you want to view

- Click the **Play** button on the **memory cover** to begin the slideshow

Changing Your Slideshow Theme

Adhere to the same instructions for beginning a slide show in memories above

- Click **any part** of the screen

- Click on the **pause** button at the bottom

- Swipe right or left on the **menu bar** right below the **slideshow** to change the theme. Changing the theme also changes the song and font for the memory title.

The **theme** is applied automatically when you make a choice.

Editing Your Title, Music, Duration, and Photos in a Memories Slideshow

- Execute the same steps for changing your slideshow theme in iOS 13 as outlined above

- Under the **theme** menu bar, you will find the **duration** options. You can make changes to the default length option if you wish

- Click **Edit** in the corner of the upper right

- Click on the **slideshow element** you want to personalize

When you are done, click on **Done** to save them

Saving a Memories Slideshow

- Use the method outlined above to make all the changes you want to make to a memories slide show

- Click on the **Share** button at bottom left corner

- Click on **Save Video**

Deleting Selected Photos from a Slideshow

- Open **Photos**

- Click on **Memories** in the menu bar at screen bottom

- Click on the **memory** you want to view

- Click on **Select** at upper right

- Select the **photos** you want to remove

- Next, click on the **garbage** can at lower right corner

  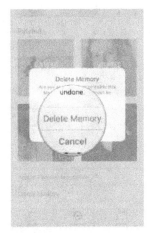

Deleting Selected Photos from a Memories Slideshow in iOS 13

Follow the first 3 steps as outlined in the steps of customizing a memories slide show above

- Next, click on **Photos & videos** in the **slideshow Edit Menu**

- Scroll through the **Photos & Video timeline** and find the photo you don't want and click on the **Delete** button to remove it from the **slideshow**

- Click **Done** to save changes

- Click a second time to save the slideshow

How to Make a Memories Slideshow a Favorite

- **Open Photos**

- Click **Memories** at bottom menu bar

- Click on the **memory** you would like to view

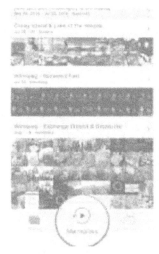

- Navigate to the bottom of the screen

- Click **Add to Favorite Memories**

How to Favorite a Memories Slideshow in iOS 13

- Open **Photos**

- Navigate to the **For You** section

- From **memories**, click **See All**

- Click on a **memory** that you want to see

- Click on the **"…."** Button at top right corner

- Click **Add to Favorites Memories**

- Return to the **All Memories** screen

- Click **Favorites** to see your favorited memories

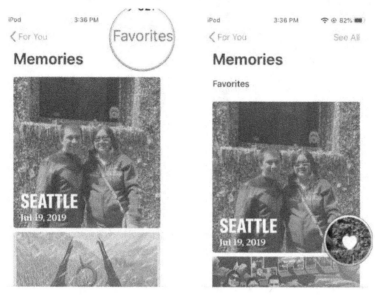

Deleting a Memories slideshow

- Open the **Photos** app

- Click on **Memories** in menu bar at screen bottom

- Click on the **memory** you would like to see

- Navigate to screen bottom

- Click **Delete Memory**

- Click **Delete Memory** a second time when you are asked to

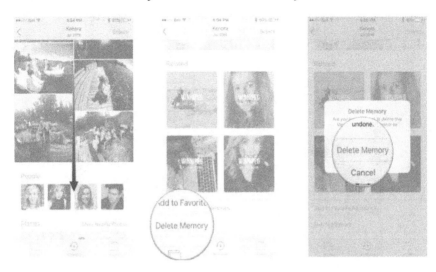

Deleting a Memories Slideshow

- Go to **photos**

- Navigate to the **For You** section

- From **Memories**, click **See All**

- Click on a **Memory** you want to see

Click on the **"..."** button at upper right corner

Click **Delete Memory**

How to View Who Was in Your Memories Slideshow

- Go to **Photos**

- Click on **Memories** in menu bar at screen bottom

- Click on the **memory** you want to view

- **Navigate down** till you see the **"Groups & People"** section

- **Swipe left and right** to see the faces that appeared in your slideshow

How to See on a Map the Location of a Specific Memories Slideshow

- Open **Photos**

- Click **Memories** in menu bar at screen bottom

- Click the **memory** you want to view

- Navigate down to the **"places"** section

- Click the **map** to view where the photos were taken

Taking a Photo

- Open the **Camera** app

- Click the **Shutter** button

- Click the **Thumbnail** button to preview and edit

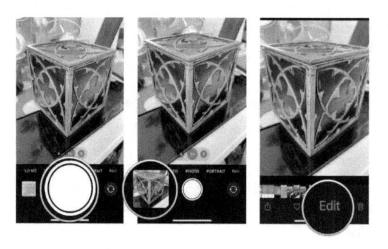

Using the Volume Button to take a Photo

- Open the **Camera** app

- Line up the scene you want to capture normally

- Next, push on the **physical volume up** button to call up the camera shutter and take a picture

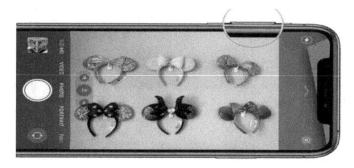

Using the Headphone Remote to take a Photo

It's possible to use your headphone as a medium to activate the camera shutter and snap photos since a lot of them come with control modules. Even if your headphone is the cord type or wireless, it's possible to use it to activate the camera shutter over a considerable distance.

- Open the **Camera** app

- Line up the scene you want to capture normally

- Next, push the **physical volume up** button on the headset to call up the shutter and take a picture

Using the Burst Mode to take and Select Photos

- Open the **Camera** app

- Line up the scene you want to capture normally

- Next, **click and hold** the shutter button or **swipe to the left** in quick succession form burst mode capture depending on model of iPhone you have

  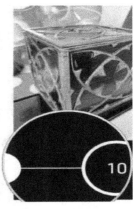

iOS will try to select what it sees as the best picture but you can make a different choice if you don't agree with iOS

- click on the **thumbnail** at bottom left corner after the burst capture

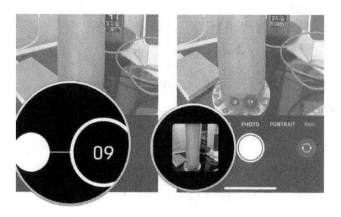

- Click on the **Burst mode stack** you want to see

- Click **Select**

- Click the **blue checkmark** on the photos you want to retain

- Click **Done** after choosing the images you want to keep

- Click **Keep Everything** if you want to keep all images in the stack or **Keep Only (number) Favorites** to delete the unwanted images.

Setting the Flash

- Open the **Camera** app

- Click the **flash icon** in the upper left corner

- Choose if you want it on **Auto, On** or **Off**

Setting the Timer

Open the **Camera** app

Tap the **arrow** at screen top or **swipe up** from above the shutter button

 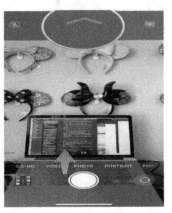

- Click the **timer** button

- Choose between **3 seconds** or **10 seconds**

- Next click the **shutter button** to begin the countdown. The screen should start blinking as it counts down.

 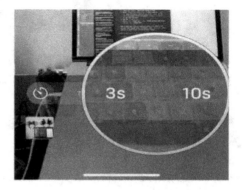

Switching in Between Cameras (front and rear facing)

- Open the **Camera** app

- Click the **flip camera button** to alternate between the front facing facetime and rear camera

- Next click the **shutter button** to shoot picture or start recording a video

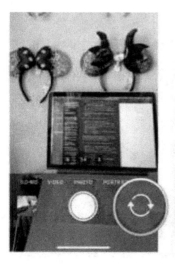 

How to take a Square Photo

- Open the **camera** app

- Click on the **arrow** at screen top or **swipe up** from above the shutter button

- Next, click on the **aspect ratio** button

- Click on **square**

How to take a Panorama

- Open the **Photo** app

- Swipe to the **left twice** to change the mode to pano

- Click the **arrow** button to change the capture direction

- Click the **shutter button** to begin taking a panoramic photo

- **Turn your device** to capture as much of your environment to your desire.

- To finish, click the **shutter button** again

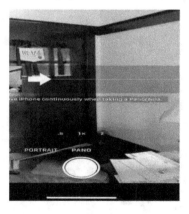 

Using live Photo Filters

- Open the **Camera** app

- Click the **arrow** at screen top or swipe up from above the shutter button

- Click the **filter** button that looks like three interlapping circles

- Choose the **filter** you want to use

Click the **shutter button** to take the photo with the filter applied

Enhancing Images in Photos

- Open the **Photos** app

- Locate the photo you want to enhance and open it

- Click on the **Edit** button in the upper right corner of the screen

- Click on the **auto-enhance button** that has the appearance of a magic wand

- You can switch between Auto-Enhance by clicking on it again to let you see before and after

- Click **Done** if you like the adjustments the Auto-Enhance feature made

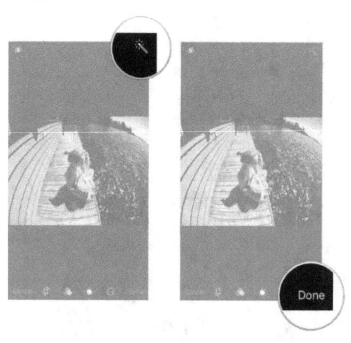

How to Enhance Photos

- Open **photos**

- Locate a photo to enhance and open it

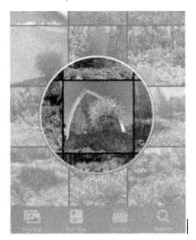

- Click **Edit** at upper right corner

- Ensure you are in the **lighting** section (a dial with dots around it) and click the **auto-enhance** button that resembles a magic wand

- You can slide the **dial** at the bottom to change the intensity of the **auto-enhance** feature. This makes changes to other aspects automatically

Click **Done** in the bottom right corner when you finish

Changing Lighting with Smart Adjustments in Photos

- Open the **photos** app
- Locate the **photo** you would like to enhance and open it
- Click on the **Edit** button at the upper right of the screen
- Click on the **adjustments** button that looks like a dial with dots around it at the bottom navigation.
- Click on **Light**
- Swipe left and right to move the **slider** to effect adjustments to your photo

- Click and hold on the **photo** to see the original so you can view it in comparison to your edited version

- Click **Done** at bottom right and your changes will be saved

Changing the lighting in your photos in iOS 13

- Open **Photos**

- Locate a **Photo** and open it

- Click **Edit** in upper right corner

- Click the **Lighting** button in the bottom menu bar
- **Swipe horizontally** to browse the various categories and click the one you want to adjust

For each adjustment you want to do, slide the **dial** at the bottom left to right for a more pronounced or less pronounced effect

- Click **Done** at bottom right corner to **save** the changes you have made

Changing Color in your Photos

- Open **photos**

- Locate the photo you want to work on and open it

- Click the **Edit** Button

- Click on the **color** button at the center of the bottom menu bar

- **Swipe** left and right to find a color filter that you like

- If you need to make further adjustments to color, click on the **lighting** button at bottom menu bar

- Choose between **Saturation, Vibrance, Warmth** and **Tint** by **swiping** left and right

- Adjust the **dial** till you are ok

- Click **Done** at bottom right to **save**

Converting Photos to Black and White

- Open **photos**

- Locate the photo and open it

- Click the **Edit** button

- Click the **color** button in the bottom menu bar

- Swipe through the filters till you get to the 3 options: **Mono, Silvertone** and **Noir**. As you click through, they are automatically applied

- If you feel the need to make any adjustments, click on the **lighting** button to make any changes to the lighting aspect

- Click **Done** to **save**

Fine-tuning with Smart Adjustments in Photos

- Open **Photos**

- **Locate and open the photo**

- Click on the **Edit** button at screen upper right

- Click on the **adjustments** button in the bottom navigation

- Click on the **dropdown arrow** next to **Color, Light,** or **B&W**

130

- Click the **name of the adjustment** you would like to make

- Use the **slider** to swipe left and right to make an adjustment
- Click and hold the photo to see the **original** to compare to the edited one
- Click **Done** at bottom right corner and **save** changes

Reverting to Original Photo

- Open **Photos**

- Locate an edited photo

- Click **Edit** at upper right corner

- Click **Revert** at bottom right

- Next, **confirm** that you want the **edited** photo rest restored to **original** form

Trimming your video

- Open **Photos and** select **Albums** at bottom of the app

- Click **Videos**

- Select the **video** you want to edit

- Click **Edit** at top right of the screen

- Click and hold on the left or right side of the **timeline** to activate the trimming tool

- Move the **anchor** left or right to trim

- Click on and hold an anchor to expand the **timeline** for more accurate editing

- Click **Done** at bottom right of screen

Resizing a Video

- Open **Photos**

- Go to **Albums** at app bottom

- Select **Videos**

- Choose the **video** to *edit*

- Click **Edit** at top right of screen

- Click on the **crop** icon

- Using your finger, choose from **Straighten, Horizontal, or Vertical**

- Move your finger left or right to resize

Flipping and Rotating a Video

- Open **photos.** Go to **Albums.** Select the **video** to edit

- Click **Edit** at top right of screen

- Click on the **crop** icon

- Select the **flip** icon at top left to flip the video

- Click the **rotate** icon at top left to rotate the video.

- Click **Done**

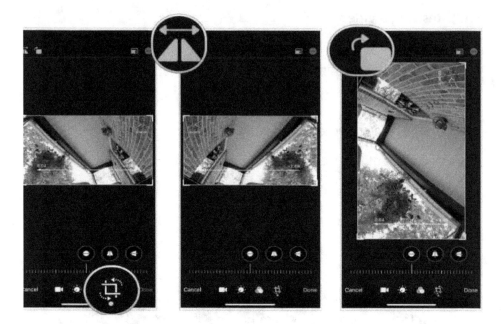

Adjusting the Video Brightness

- Open **Photos. Go** to **Albums.** Select **Videos**

- Choose the **video** to edit and click **Edit** at top right of screen

- Click on the **adjustment** icon and select the **brightness** circle

- You can move left and right to select a **brightness level**

- Click **Done**

Adjusting the Video Saturation

- Open **Photos.** Go to **Albums.** Select **Videos**

- Choose the **video** to edit and click **edit** at top right of screen

- Click the **adjustment** icon

- Select the **saturation** circle

- Move left and right to select the **saturation** point

- Click **Done**

To Further Adjust Your Video

- Open **Photos. Go** to **Albums.** Select **Videos**

- Choose the **video** to edit and click **Edit** at top right of the screen

- Click the **icon** for your desired solution

- Move left and right to choose a **setting you wish to alter**

- Click **Done.**

 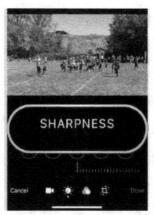 

Adding a Video Filter

- Open **photos.** Go to **Albums.** Select **Videos**

- Choose the **video** to edit

- Click **Edit** at top right

- Click on the **filter** icon

- From under, move left and right to change the **filter setting**

- Click **Done**

Muting video Sounds

- Open **photos.** Go to **Albums.** Select **videos**

- Choose the **video** to edit

- Click **Edit** at top right

- Click the **sound** icon at the top left to turn it on or off

- Click **Done**

Using Filters in the Photos App

- Open **photos**

- Click on the **photo** to apply filter

- Click **Edit** button at top right of screen

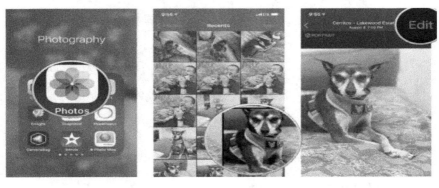

- Click the **filters** button at middle of bottom menu

- Move and click on the **filter** you want to apply

- Click **Done**

 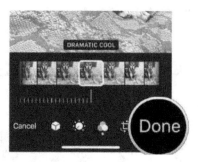

Rotating Photos

- Open **photos**

- Find and open the **photo**

- Click on **Edit** at top right corner

- Click on the **crop** button at bottom menu

- The **rotate** button looks like a box with a curved arrow. Click on it to rotate the photo till you get your desired alignment

- Click **Done** to save changes

To Straighten Photos

- Open **Photos**

- Find and open a **photo**

- Click **Edit** at upper right corner

- Next, click the **crop** button at bottom menu

Normally, it goes to **straighten**. Drag you finger along the dial at bottom to straighten out the image

You can still click on the **Vertical** or **Horizontal** options if you want the photo in any of those alignments

- Adjust the **slider** till you are happy with the results
- Click **Done** to save changes

Cropping Photos

- Open **Photos**
- Find and open the **photo**
- Click **Edit** in upper right corner
- Click the **crop** button at bottom menu

 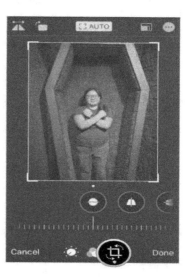

- Click and drag on the **corner handles** of the crop till you are happy with the results

- Click **Done** to save changes

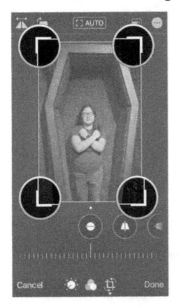

Changing the Aspect Ratio in Photos

- Open **Photos**

- Find and open the **photo**

- Click **Edit** at top right of the screen

- Click on the **crop** icon at bottom menu

- Next, click on the **aspect ratio** button at lower right of screen

- Move your finger on the **dial** to center the photo to your liking

- Click **Done** when you are done

Changing the Aspect Ratio

- Open **photos.** Find and open the photo

- Click **Edit** at top right corner and click the **crop** button

- Click the **Aspect Ratio** button at the top. Its yellow in color and next to the 3 dots in a circle

- **Swipe** horizontally to scroll through the aspect ratio options

- Click the **ratio** you want to use

- Click **Done** to save changes

Turning on Photo and Video Extensions in Photos in the Photo app

- Open the **Photos** app

- Click on the photo or video you want to edit

- Click **Edit** at upper right corner

 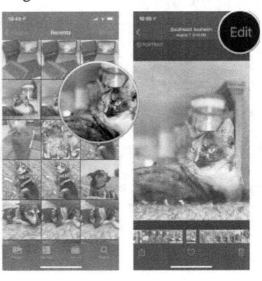

- Click on the **"..."** button at upper right corner

- Click on **More** in the menu

- Click on **Edit**

- Next, click the **green circle with a white cross in the middle** on the extensions you want to favorite and you can rearrange the order they appear by moving the handle on the right

Accessing and Using Photo and Video Extensions in the Photos app

- Follow steps 1-4 as outlined in how to turn on photo and video extensions in photos app above

- Next, tap on the **extension** you want to use

- Do your editing

- Click **Done** to save changes

Assigning Pictures to Contacts Via the Photo App

- Open the **Photos** app

- Click the **album** that contains the photo you want to use for your contacts photo

- Click on the specific photo and open it

- Next, click on the **Share** button at bottom left corner

- Locate and click **Assign to contact** on bottom menu

- Click on the **contact** that you would like to assign the photo to

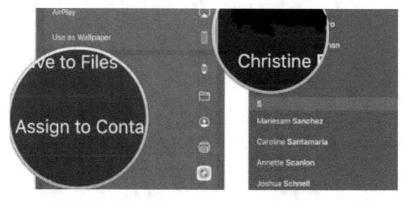

- Set the **scale** of the photo you want to use to ensure it fits the frame

- Click **Update** to save changes

 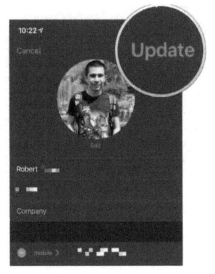

Using the Photo App to set Your Wall paper

- Open **the Photo** app

- Open the **album** you would like to use in the slideshow

- Click on and open the **photo** you would like to use to open it

- Click on the **Share** button at bottom left corner

- Locate and click **Use as Wallpaper** at bottom menu

148

- Click **Set** and choose the screen to which you would apply the wallpaper. You can choose **Set Lock screen, Set Home Screen** or **click** on **Set Both**

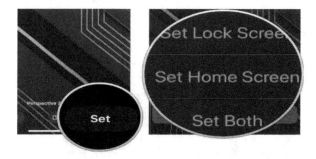

Starting a Slideshow with the Photos App

- Open **Photos**

- Click on an **album** or the **photos** icon

- Click **Select**

- Select the **photos** you want in your slideshow

- Click the **Share** button at bottom left

- Click on **Slideshow**. It should start at once

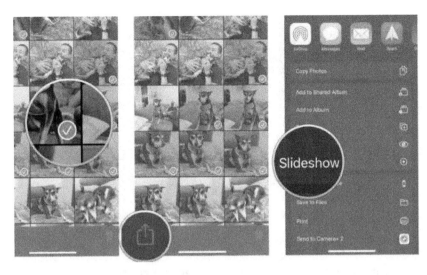

Playing a Whole Album as a Slide Show

- Open **Photos**

- Click the **album** you want to play as a slide show

- Click the **album** name and **date range**

- Click on the **play** button

Airplaying Your photos to Your TV

- Open the **Photos** app

- Click on the **photo** or **video** you want to share

- Click on the **Share** button at bottom left corner

- Click **Airplay**

- Next, click on the **Apple TV** or **Airplay-compatible Tv** to which you would like to share the photo or video

Sharing Individual Photos or Videos Using Photos

- Open the **Photos** app

- Click on the **photo** or **video** you want to share

- Click on the **Share** button at bottom left corner

- Click on the sharing **method**

How to share individual photos or videos in iOS 13

- Open **Photos**

- Locate a specific **photo** or **video** to share

- Click on the **Share** button at bottom right

- Choose the sharing method

Sharing Multiple Photos

- Open **Photos**

- Find the **photos** or **videos** to share

- Click **Select** at top right

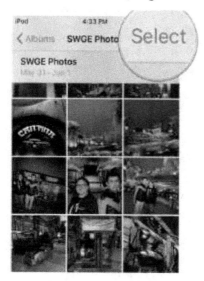

- Click on the **photos** or videos to share. In the alternative, you can drag your fingers across rows and columns for faster selection

- Click **Share**

- Choose your sharing method

Printing Photos

- Open **Photos**

- Click on the **photo** you want to print

- Click on the **Share** button at lower left corner

- **Swipe** to the left from the bottom menu to view the **print** option

- Next, click on **Print**

- Click **Select Printer**

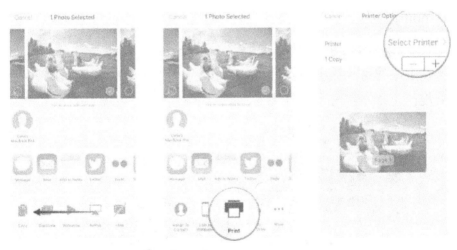

- Click on the specific **printer** you want to use

- Use the **+ or –** buttons to specify the number of copies

- Click **Print**

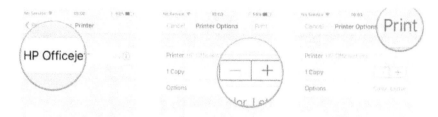

Using Siri to Locate Photos Based on Time

Push **the Home** or **Side button** to activate siri or you can say **"Hey Siri"**

You can say something like: **"show me photos from March"**

You can choose to be more **specific** by mentioning a **particular date** not just month for better accuracy

Using Siri to Find Photos Based on Location

Push and hold the **Home** or **Side button** to activate **siri or say "Hey Siri"**

You can now say something like **"show me photos from California"**

Using Siri to Find Photos of Things

Press and hold the **Home** or **side button** to activate Siri or you can say

"Hey siri"

You can now say something like, **"show me photos of airplanes"**

Searching for Photos in the Photos App

- Open the **Photo**s app

- Click the **Search** icon at bottom right corner

- From the search screen you can choose to search the following:

- **Moments, People, Places, Categories** and **Groups**

Using the Search Bar to Find What you Want in the Photos App

- Click the **Search Bar** at the top of the Search section

- **Enter** the keywords you want to search for

- Click **Search** on the keyboard when Done

Using Names to Make People Easier to Locate in the Photos App

- Open **Photos**

- Click **Albums**

- Navigate down and select the people **album**

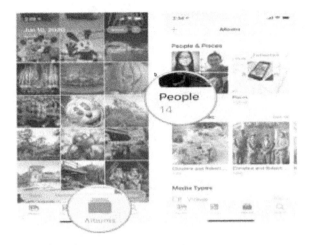

- Click on any **unnamed people** to see images of that person

- From the top, click **Add** name to give them a name

- Click **Next.** Click **Done**

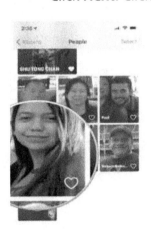

Chapter 13: Music

The music app is great for finding great music and building your playlists. You can download music, get music from the Apple music service and Beats 1 radio. Here's how you can make great use of the music function of your device:

Adding songs to music

You have 3 options:

- You can buy music from iTunes store. The songs would automatically be added to your music app. You can also download purchased songs via iCloud if you used another device to buy music.

- You can add music via the Apple music catalog. You do this clicking on the More button next to a track and then clicking Add to my music

- You can also get music by iTunes Sync

  ### Locating Songs in Music
- Click on the **magnifying glass** at top right

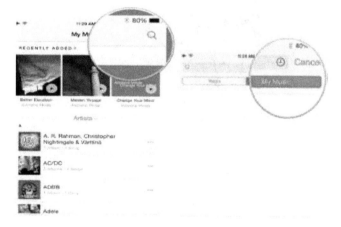

- Next, click on the **My Music** at top right

- Type the song name, artist or album

To Go to Recent Searches to Locate Something:

- Click on the **magnifying glass** at top right

- Click on the **clock** icon at right of the search bar

- Click any **recent result** to repeat the search

- Click **Clear** at top left and tap **Clear Recent Searches** to remove the results list

Browsing for Songs in Music

- Click on the **My Music** tab

- Click on the **category** button at the top of the song list

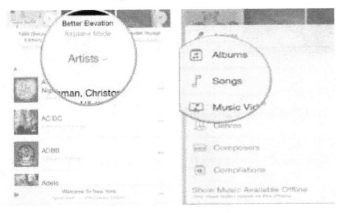

- Click on the category you want to sort either by **Albums, Songs, Music, Videos, Genres, Composers,** or **Compilations**

How to Download Songs

- Click the **More** button that looks like 3 dots to the right of the artist, album, playlist or song

- Click on the **Make Available Offline** button

- Click on the **Downloads** tab to view and organize the caching. When a music is available for offline playback, you would see a small **device icon** at top right of the More button

To Remove Downloaded Songs from Cache

- Click the **More** button to the right of the artist, album, or song you want to expel

- Click the **Remove Download** button

- When the music is removed from the local cache, the **device icon** will not be in evidence at its former place at top right of the More button

Deleting songs from your music library

- Click on the **More** button to the right of the artist, album or song

- Click on **delete**

- Click the **Delete purchase** button

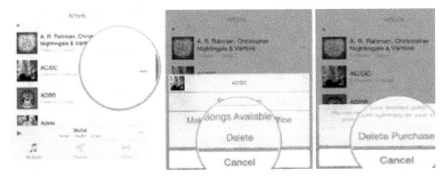

Accessing playlists

- Click the **My Music** tab at bottom right

- Click the **playlist** tab at the top

Playing a playlist

- Click on the **name** of a playlist to play it immediately

- You can click the **More** button and then click "play Next" to include it to the beginning of your Up Next queue

- You can also click **More** button, then click to **Add to Up Next** to add it to the end of your Up Next queue

Creating a New Playlist

- Click **new**

- Type a **title**

- Click the **Camera** icon to select a thumbnail

- Type a **description**

- Click **Add Songs** to begin adding songs

- Click **Done** at top right to end

Adding Tracks to a Playlist

- Click **Edit**

- Click **Add songs**

- **Search** out the tracks or songs you want to include
- Click the + button to add the track
- Click **Done** at top right to end

In case you want to add tracks from any location in the music app:

- Click on the **More** button to the right of the track you want to add
- Click **Add to playlist**
- Click on the **playlist** you want to add it to

Arranging Tracks on a playlist

- Open the **playlist**

- Click **Edit**

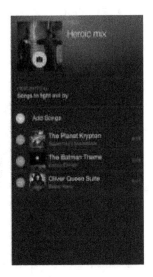

- Tap and hold down on the **grabber** button to the right of the track you want to move

- Drag the **track** to its new position

- Click **Done** at top right to end

Removing a Track from a Playlist

Locate the **playlist**

- Click on **Edit.** Click the **red –** button to right of the track

- Click the red **Delete** button

Deleting a playlist

Click on the **More** button to the right of the playlist

Click **Delete**

Click **delete playlist** to confirm

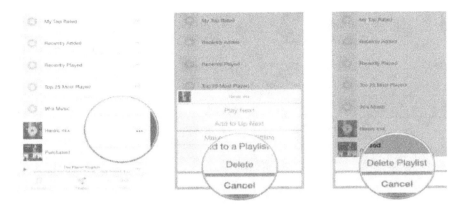

It's possible to delete a playlist from the specific playlist screen itself:

- Click the **More** button

- Click **Delete**

- Click **Delete** playlist to confirm

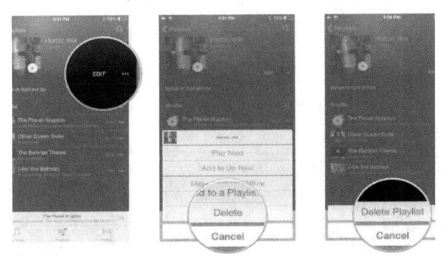

Creating a Genius Playlist

iTunes can do your mixing and matching if you let it. It will accomplish this via the iTunes algorithm. If it's not turned on by default, you can engage it yourself:

- Open **Settings**

- Click on **Music**

- Switch **Genius** to on and **Accept** the terms and conditions

- Click on the **More** button to the right of a song

- Click on **Create Genius Playlist**

Using Up Next

This is a feature that allows you listen to music you suddenly want to hear without disrupting what you initially had lined up.

Quickly Add Music to up Next from Anywhere

- Locate the **track, album** or **playlist**

- Click the **More** button

- Click on **play Next** to add the music to the front of your Up Next queue or **Add to Up Next** to place it at the end of the queue

How to Quickly clear Up Next from Anywhere

- Locate the **track, album** or **playlist**

- Click on the **track, album** or **playlist** to begin playing it

- Click **Clear Up Next** from the menu

To view Your Up Next Queue

- Find the **mini player** just above the bar

- Click the **track information** button on the mini player to call up the now Playing screen

- Click on the **Up Next** button

- Click the **Done** button

Viewing Your Up Next History

- From the **Up Next** screen

- Swipe down to show your **Up Next history**

- Click a **track** if you wish to hear it again

- Click **Done**

Adding music to Up Next

- From the **Up Next** screen

- Click on **Add**

- **Search** for the music you wish to include

- Click the+ on the right to add a track, playlist or album

Re-arranging What's Up Next

- From the **Up Next** screen

- Tap and hold the **grabber** button to the right of the track you want to move

- Move the track to the desired position

Removing a Track from Up Next

- From the **Up Next** screen

- Swipe to the left on the **track** to show the red Remove button

- Click the red **Remove** button

Clearing Music from Up Next

- Open the **Up Next** screen

- Click on **clear** at the top

- Click **Up Next** at the bottom to confirm.

Chapter 14: Mail

Setting Up Mail on Your Device

- Open **Settings**

- Click **Accounts & Passwords**

- Click **Add Account**

- Click **Google**

- Click **continue** if asked to confirm that you want to allow Google.com to sign in on your device

- Type your **Google account** details

- Ensure that the **toggles** for mail, contacts and calendars are in the "on" or "off" positions depending on the settings you want

- Click **Save**

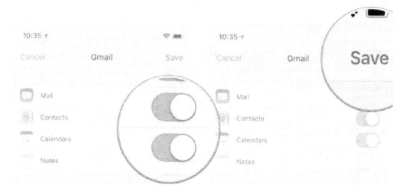

Setting Up Outlook.com Mail
- Repeat step 1-3 as above (setting up mail)

- Click **Outlook.com**

- Type your **Outlook.com account details**

- Repeat steps 9 and 10 above (setting up mail)

Setting up Exchange Mail
- Repeat steps 1-3 as above

- Click **Exchange**

- Type your **Exchange email address**

- Click **Next**

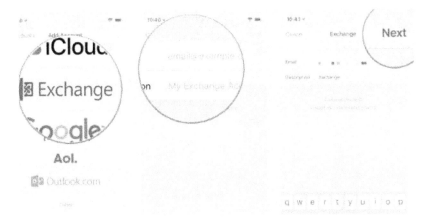

- Click **Configure Manually**

- Type your **Exchange account information** if you chose to configure your account manually

- Click **Next**

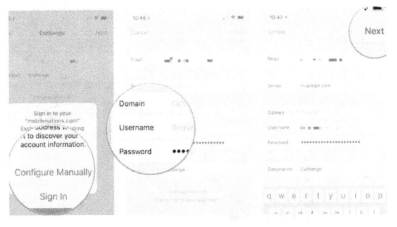

- Repeat step 9 and 10 above

Setting Up IMAP/POP, CalDav and CardDAV

- Follow steps 1-3 as above

- Click **Other**

- Choose the **type** of account you want to configure. Choose mail for an email account CalDAV for a calendar and CardDAV for contacts

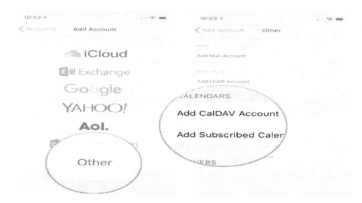

- Type your **account information**
- Click **Next**
- Click **Done**

Setting Up a Default Email
- Open **Settings**
- Click **Mail**
- Navigate down and click **Default Account**
- Click the **account** you would like to use as default

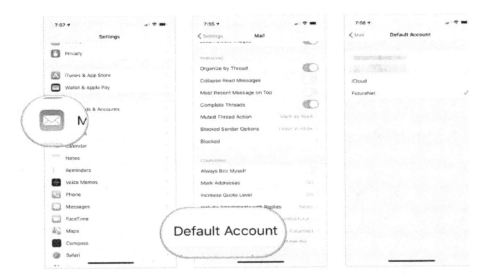

Switching Between Email Accounts

- Open **Mail**
- Click the **Compose** button
- Click the **From field**
- Click the **account** from the picker that you would like to use and the mail will be sent from the selected account

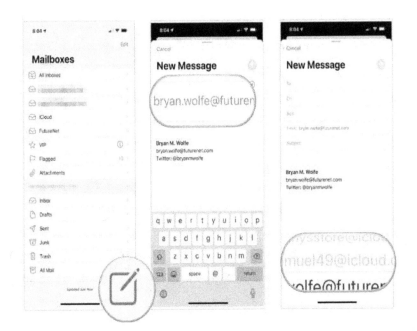

Disabling an Email Account

- Open **Settings**

- Click **Passwords & Accounts**

- Click the **account** you want to disable

- Switch **Mail** off

Deleting an Email Account

- Open **Settings**

- Click **Passwords & accounts**

- Click the **account** you want to delete

- Click **Delete Account**

Getting New Mail Notifications

- Open **Settings**

- Click on **Notifications** and navigate up until you get to mail

- Click on **Mail**

- Click on the **switch** beside **Allow Notifications**

- Click on the **mail** you wish to adjust its notification settings

You can decide to adjust and customize your notifications to add sounds, notifications in the notifications center, badge app icons, etc.

Managing Small Accounts

Open **Settings**

Navigate to **Passwords & Accounts**

Click the **account** you would like to manage and adjust your email account

Changing Preview Lines

- Go to **Settings**

- Click **Mail**

- Select **Preview** and select the number of lines to alter the mail preview display

Displaying To/Cc Labels

- Go to **Settings**

- Click **Mail**

- Click the **switch** next to Show To/Cc Labels so it would change to a green color

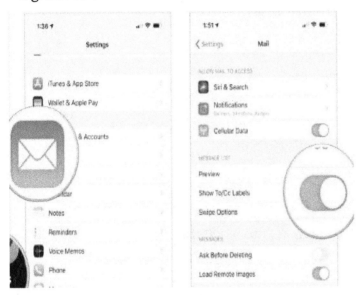

Adjusting Swipe Options

- Open **Settings**

- Click **Mail**

- Click **Swipe Options**

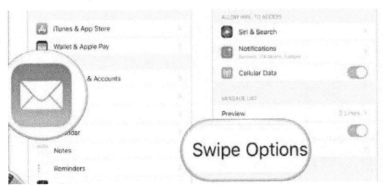

- Click **Swipe Left** or **Swipe Right** to change the slide options

- Click **flag** or **Move Message** to set the slide direction

How to toggle Ask Before Deleting

- Open the **Settings** app

- Click **Mail**

- Click the **switch** next to **Ask Before Deleting** so it would become green

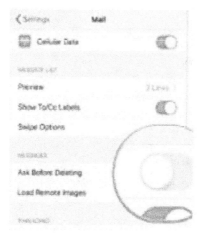

Loading Remote Images

- Open **Settings**

- Click **Mail**

- Click the **switch** next to **Load Remote Images**

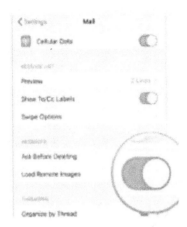

Organizing Emails by Thread

- Open **settings**

- Click **mail**

- Click on the **switch** next to **Organize by Thread**

Collapsing Read Messages

- Open **Settings**

- Click **Mail**

- Click the **switch** next to **collapse Read Massages**

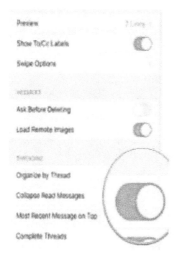

Moving a Thread's Most Recent Message to the Top

- Open **Settings**

- Click **Mail**

- Click the **switch** next to **Most recent Message in Top**

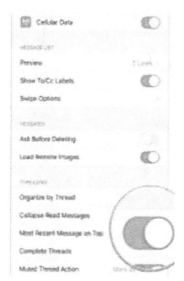

Turning Complete Threads on and Off

- Open **Settings**

- Click **Mail**

- Click the switch next to **Complete Threads**

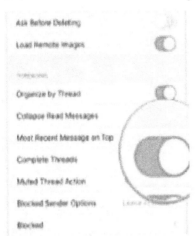

How to Turn Always Bcc Myself on and off

- Open **Settings**

- Click **Mail**

- Click the **switch** next to **Always Bcc Myself**

Marking Addresses

- Open **Settings**

- Click **Mail**

- Click **Mark Addresses**

- Enter the **type of address** you would like to mark

Turning Increase Quote Level on and off

- Open **Settings.** Click **Mail.** Click **Increase Quote level**

- Click the **switch** next to **Increase Quote Level**

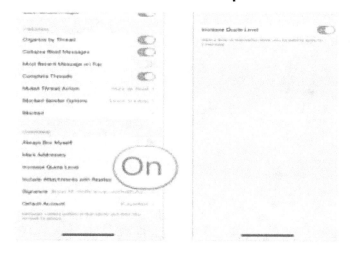

Setting Your Signature

- Open **Settings**

- Click **Mail**

- Click **Signature**

- Add your **new signature**

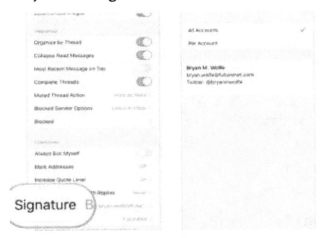

Mark an Email as Read or Unread

- Open the **Mail app**

- Click **Edit** at upper right

- Select any **mail** you would like to mark as read

- Click **Mark** at lower left corner

- Click **Mark as Read** and if the messages you selected have been read, you can click **Mark as Unread**

Flagging an Email

- Open the **Mail app**

- Click **Edit** at upper right

- Select the **message** you like to flag

- Click **Mark** at lower left of your screen

- Click **Flag** and if the message you selected was already flagged, you can click **Unflag**

Adding New Mailboxes

- Open the **Mail** app

- Click **Edit** at upper right

- Select **New Mailbox** at lower right corner

- Enter a name for your mailbox in the **Name** field

- Click the **Mailbox Location** field to attach your new folder to an account

- Select a **main mailbox** in which you would like to locate your new mailbox

Moving Messages to Different Mailboxes

- Open the **Mail app**

- Select the **mailbox** where the message you want to move is located

- Click **Edit**

- Choose the **message** you want to move

- Select **Move**

- Choose the **mailbox** to which you would like to move the message

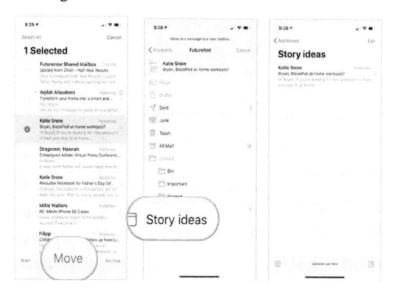

Adding Contacts to Your VIP List

- Open **Mail app**

- Select the **VIP** under your normal inbox

- Click **Add VIP**

- Select a person from your contacts list to add to the VIP list

- You can still select Add VIP to add more

Filtering Inboxes in the Mail App

- Open the **mail app**

- From **Mailboxes,** select your mail account

- Click an **inbox**

- Select the **filter** button at left corner of the screen

- Click **Filtered By**

- Choose the **category** to be filtered

- Click **Done** at upper right part of the screen

Unsubscribing to Mailing Lists

- Open the **Mail app**

- Choose an **email** from a mailing list that you don't want to receive anymore

- Click **Unsubscribe** at the top of the mail

- Select **Unsubscribe** when asked to confirm

Creating a New Email in the Mail App

- Open the **Mail app**

- Click the **Compose** button

- Enter the **recipient email address** or name of the person that the mail is intended for

- Select the **subject field** and add the subject of the mail

- Click the **message field** and type the message

- When you are done, click **Send** at top right corner

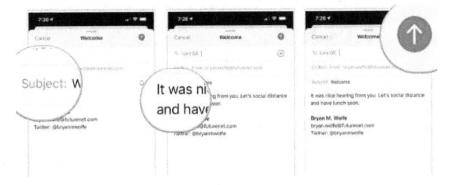

Choosing an Email Address from Your Contacts in the Mail App

- Open the **Mail app**

- Click the **Compose** button at bottom right corner of screen

- Select the + sign in the circle ** to call up your contacts

- Choose the **contact** you would like to add and they would be automatically included to the mail

How to access drafts in the mail app

Open the **Mail** app

Click on and hold the **Compose** button at lower right corner and the drafted emails would be brought up

Select the **email draft** you want to edit and send when you are done

Using Siri to Send Email

- Push and hold the home button or say" **Hey Siri"** to engage the feature

- Next you can say **"send an email to John"**

- If siri presents you with more than one option, you will have to click on the correct one or you could give the command with specifics that would enable siri to identify the correct recipient

- Next, let Siri know the **email subject**

- Let Siri know the **email content**

- Allow Siri to **confirm the email content**

- Click **Send** or say **Yes** to send the email. If you have issues with the mail, you can either tell Siri to change any aspect of it or cancel it entirely

 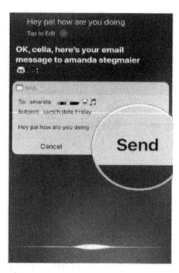

Making Siri Read Your Unread Emails
- Push and hold the Home button or say **Hey Siri** to activate it

- Next, ask it to **"Read my unread emails"**

- Click on any email to see it in the app

Asking Siri to Respond to an Email

- Open the **Mail app**

- Click on in**box**

- Click on the **mail** you want to respond to

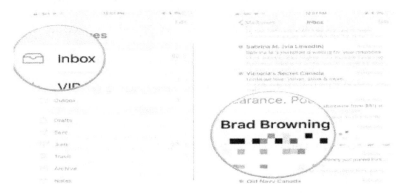

- Push and hold the **Home button** or say **"Hey Siri"** to activate it

- Next, ask Siri to **"Respond to this mail"**

- Let siri know what you want the **email to say**

Using Siri to Create a Contact Relationship

- To be able to do this, you will have to let siri know your relationships so the voice assistant would be able to serve you well. You have to let siri know who your wife or husband is, boss, best friend, children etc. you have two ways. You could either edit the information or tell siri verbally

- Push and hold the **Home button** or say **"Hey Siri"** to wake the voice assistant up

- Let siri know the relationship making sure to say the name as you saved it in your contacts. For e.g. **john smith is my boss**

- Respond with **Yes** or click **Yes** when Siri seeks a confirmation. The voice assistant will also let you know that the relationship has been added

Adding a New Email Address to a Contact in the Mail App

- Launch the **Mail app**

- Click the **email** with the new contact

- Click the **email address**

- Click **Add to existing contacts** and choose a contact

- You can equally click **Update contact** if it's labeled under the correct name

- Click **Update** at upper right corner of screen

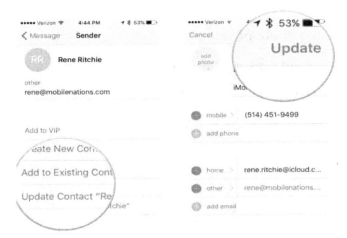

Inserting a Photo or Video into an Email in the Mail App

- Open the **Mail app**

- Click on **Compose** button at bottom right corner

- Enter the **sender info, subject, and body fields** just as you would for a regular email

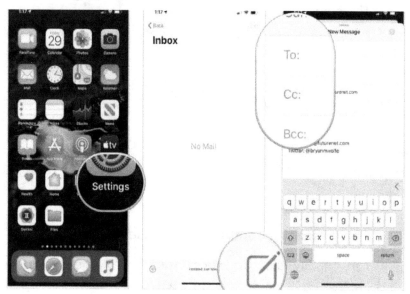

- Click in **body** and a menu will appear

- Select the **photo icon**

- Choose the **photo** or **video** you would like to insert

- Click the **send** button at upper right corner when you are done composing the mail

Adding an Attachment to a Mail

- Open the **Mail app**

- Click on the **Compose** button at bottom right

- Enter the **sender info, subject and body** fields like a regular email

- Click in the **body** and a menu will appear

- Select the **Attachment icon**

- Choose the **file** you want to send

- Click **send** at upper right when you are done composing the email

Saving a Mail as PDF in Mail

- Launch the **Mail app**

- Click an **email** you want to save as PDF

- Select the **action** button

- Navigate down and click **Print** to open the printer options

- Pinch open the **thumbnail** of the first page of your email

- Click the **Share** button at upper right corner of screen

- Choose the **app** you want to save or share your PDF converted email to

Chapter 15: Contacts

Adding a Contact to Your Device

- Open the **Contacts** app

- Click on the + sign at top right corner

- From the top section, you can enter all the necessary information like

- Contact's first name. Contact's last name. Contact's company

- Click on the **green + symbol** next to add phone number

- Key in the contact's **phone number**

- Click on **Done** at top right to save the contact

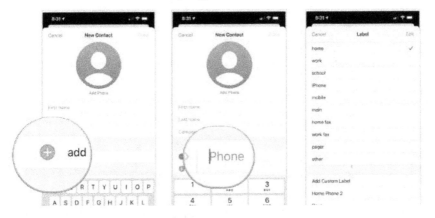

Updating an Existing Contact

- Open the **Contacts** app

- Click on the **contact** you want to update

- Click on the **Edit** button at top right corner

- You can now add any other information such as phone numbers, email address etc

Finding an Existing Contact

- Open the **Contacts** app

- Click on the **search bar**

- Enter the **contact's name** to find them

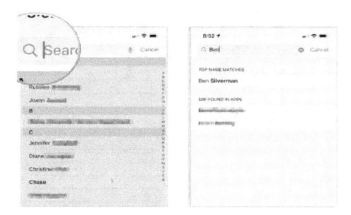

If it just so happens that you can't remember a contact's name but you are sure it's in your contact, you can find it by the first letter in their name.

- Open the **Contacts** app

- Click on a **letter** at right side of your screen

Sharing a Contact

- Go to the **Contacts** app

- Click on the **contact** you want to share

- Click on **Share Contact**

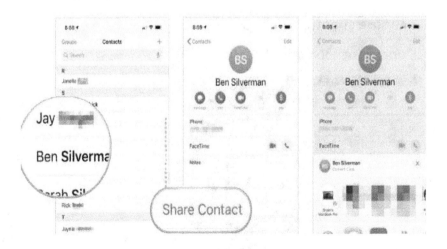

There are different ways to share the contact and you will have to use the one best suited for your intentions and follow the directions to send.

Assigning Photos to Contacts

- Open the **photos app**
- Click the **photo** you want to assign to a contact
- Click the **Share** button at bottom left of your screen
- Click on **Assign to Contact**

- Click on the **contact** you want to assign the photo to
- Next, drag and pinch the **photo** to scale and set it as you like
- Click **choose** at bottom right of screen
- Click **update** at top right of screen

Deleting a Contact

- Open the **Contacts** app

- Click on the **contact** you want to delete

- Click **Edit** at top right corner

- Navigate down to the **bottom of the page**

- Click on **Delete contact**

- Repeat step 6 again

Chapter 16: Calendar

With calendar, it's easier to organize your appointments, share agendas, invite family, friends and colleagues to events and never forget important the important stuff. Calendar is compatible with iCloud, Google calendar, Microsoft Outlook etc.

Set up

Everyone has an existing email account with contact and calendar for organizing their daily appointments. All you need do is sign in to your account and open mail, calendar or contacts on your device and everything is automatically synced.

Changing the Default Time Zone for Calendar Alerts

- Open **Settings**
- Click **Calendar**

- Click **Time zone override**
- Turn on the **Time Zone Override** switch
- Click **Time zone**

- Find the **city** you want to change the time zone to
- Click the **city** to change the default time zone for your calendar app

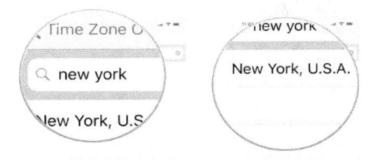

Selecting an Alternate Calendar
- Open **Settings**
- Click **Calendar**
- Click **Alternate Calendars**
- Choose between **Chinese, Hebrew or Islamic**

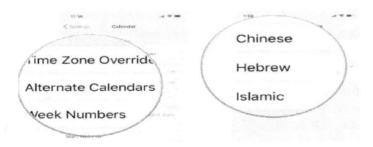

Managing Calendar Syncing

- Open the **Settings app**

- Click **Calendar**

- Click **Sync**

- Select the **time frame** you want to sync back to

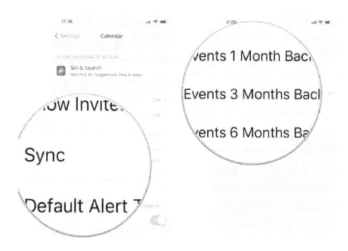

Setting Default Alert Times

- Open the **settings app**

- Click **calendar**

- Click **Default Alert Times**

- Choose the **alert** you want to set a default time for

- Specify the **time** you want to get the alert

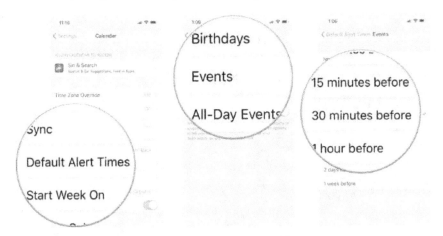

Setting a Reminder to Leave on Time

- Open **settings**

- Click **Calendar**

- Click **Default Alert Times**

- Switch **the Time to Leave** button on

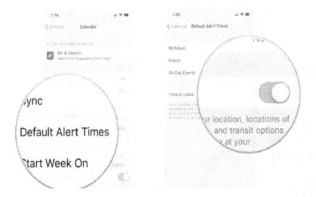

Setting the start of Your Week

- Open **Settings**

- Click **Calendar**

- Click **Start Week On**

- Click a **day of the week**

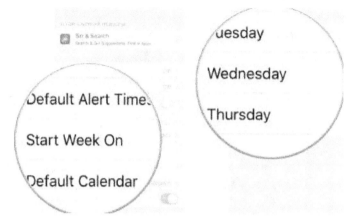

Setting a Default Calendar
- Open **Settings**

- Click **Calendar**

- Click **default calendar**

- Choose the **calendar** you want to be the default

How to turn events in Apps on and off

- Open **Settings**

- Click **Calendar**

- Click **Siri & Search**

- Next, turn **Search & Siri Suggestions** on or off
- Switch **Find Events in Other Apps** on or off based on your preferences

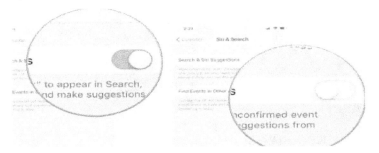

Creating a Calendar Event

- Open the **Calendar** app
- Click the + symbol at upper right-hand corner
- Type a **title, date** and **time** to your event

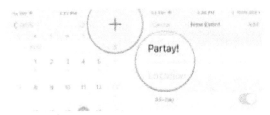

- Decide if you want the event to be an **all-day event.** If the event is time bound, you can turn the option off
- You can customize the calendar event in case it holds often.
- Click **Repeat**
- Select **how frequently** your event will repeat

- Select an alert if you want to be notified of an event

- Click **Alert**

- Specify when you want to be alerted

- Type a **URL** if there is a website associated with your event

- Click **Add** at upper right-hand corner to save your entry

Editing a Calendar Event
- Open the **Calendar** app

- Click the **day** on which your event takes place

- Click on the **event** you want to edit

- Click on **Edit** at upper right-hand corner

- You can now change anything you want to and click **Done** when you are through

Deleting a Calendar Event

- Open the **Calendar** app

- Click on the **month** or **day** the event is to hold

- Click the **event** you want to delete

- Click on **Delete Event** at the bottom of the screen

- Click **Delete Event** again to confirm. If it's a repeating event, you want to choose to **Delete This Event Only** or **Delete All Future Events**

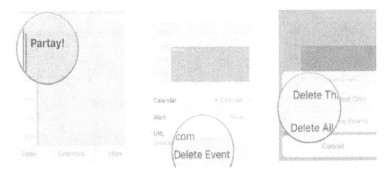

Moving a Calendar Event or Appointment by Dragging and Dropping

- Open the **Calendar** app

- Switch the list view to **off** if it's not already

- Click on the specific **day** you need to move things around for

- Click and hold on the **event** you need to change the time for.

- Next, drag the **event** to the time you need to move it to and **release it** when it's at the correct time

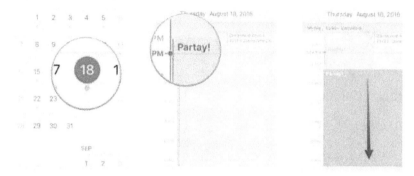

Sharing an Event

- Open the **Calendar** app

- You have the option of **creating a new event** or **click on an existing event** you want to share

- Click on the **Edit** button

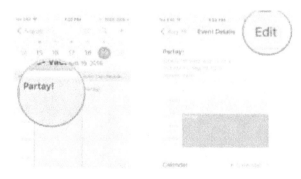

- Click on **Invitees**

- Next, **Add** all the email addresses of the recipients
- You have to do this for anyone you want to invite
- Click **Done** at upper right

Creating a Calendar Event with Siri

- Engage siri via holding down the **Home or Power button** or you can say **"Hey Siri"**
- Let siri know what you want to schedule along with details like day or date, event, and time
- Siri would now display a preview of your event and ask for your confirmation
- Should you not be satisfied with the event details, you can ask siri to **Change** to edit the information
- If you change your mind, you can **cancel**
- If you want it included to your calendar, reply with a **Yes** when siri needs a confirmation

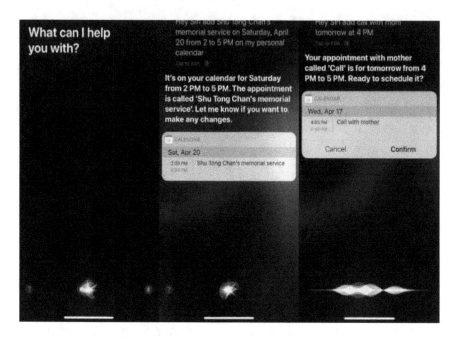

Using Siri to Update a Calendar Event

- Engage Siri with **Home or Power button** or just say **"Hey Siri"**

- Let siri know that you want to move or reschedule an event

- If you have more than one event in a day, siri would ask you to specify the event you want to make changes to

- Next, let siri know the details to be modified

- Siri would ask you for a confirmation after you have given it the new details. You are to reply **Yes** or click the button

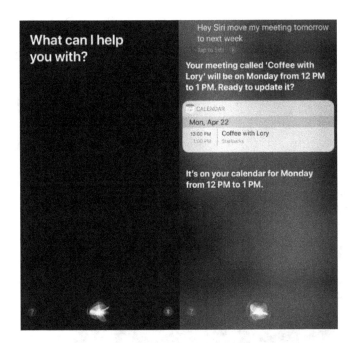

Using Siri to View and Check Your Calendar

- Engage siri with the **Home or Power** button or just say **"Hey Siri"**

- Ask siri something like: "what's my schedule like for today"

- Siri would now reply to your inquiry and read them if there are as well as display the event (s)

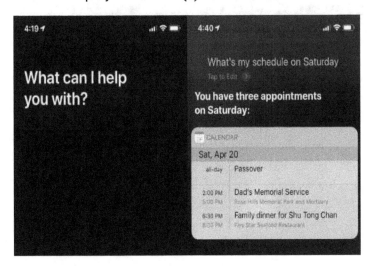

Using Siri to Cancel a Calendar Event

- Engage Siri by pushing and holding the **Home** or **Power button** or say **"Hey Siri"**

- Let siri know the event you want to cancel

- Next, siri would ask for a confirmation of what you just told it. Reply with **Yes**

Chapter 17: Maps

With apple maps, you get everything you need to get to where you are going including taking scenic routes and finding interesting places on your way. With Apple Maps, you can know your exact location, the direction you are facing, what's close to you and how to skirt around traffic. There's much more.

Viewing and Sharing Your Current Location

- Click on **Maps**
- Select the **location icon** at top right of the app

Marking Your Current Location

- Click on your **current position** in the Maps app
- Select **Mark My Location**

Sharing Your Current Location

- Click on your **current location** in the **Maps** app

- Select **Share My Location**

- Choose **how to share** your position from the choices in the share sheet

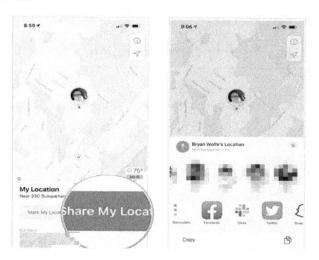

Changing Your Map View

- Click on the **Maps** app

- Locate the **location** you want to map

- Click on the **information** icon at the top right

- Select from **Maps, Transit** and **Satellite** as your view

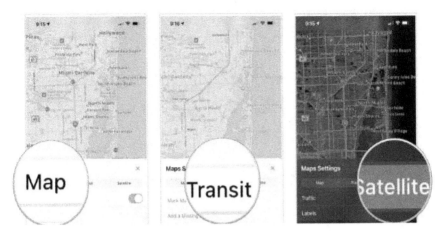

Browsing or Searching a Location

- Click on the **Maps** app

- You can use the **Search box** to locate a place or address

- Click on the **location** to see it on a map

- Select **Directions** to path your trip if needed

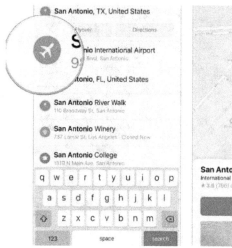

Finding Nearby Locations

- Click on the **Maps** app

- Select the **location icon** at top right of the app so the map would be centered on your location

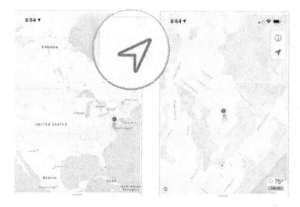

- Select the **Search box**

- Select from the several **categories** under find nearby

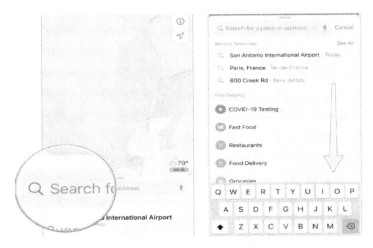

- Click on a **location** found under your chosen category

- Select **Directions** for information on to get to the place from your current position

Selecting a Route in Maps

- Click on **Maps**

- With the **Search box,** find a place or address

- Select **Directions** to path the trip

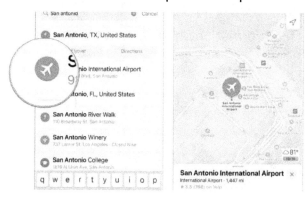

- Choose the **path** on the map that you want to take

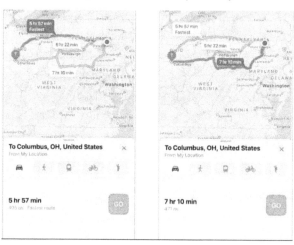

Viewing Recent Map Searches

- Open the **Maps** app

- Click on the **search bar** at screen bottom

- Select the **previous location** on the list

Adding Favorite Locations in Maps

- Open the **Maps** app

- Locate the **location** you want to favorite via the following methods:

- Enter the address in the search bar

- Dropping a pin

- Tapping on a location in the map

- From the **lower panel,** swipe upwards

- Tap on **Add favorite**

Viewing Favorite Places in Maps

- Open the **Maps app**

- Navigate down and from favorites, tap **See All**

Deleting Favorites from Maps

- Open the **Maps app**

- Navigate down and from favorites, tap **See All**

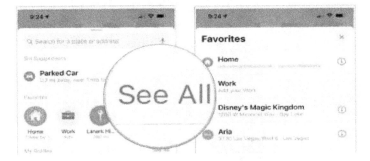

- Navigate to the left on the **location to delete**

- Press **Delete**

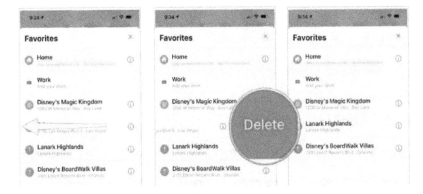

Sharing Directions with Maps

- Open the **Maps** app

- Click the **search bar**

- Type an **address or location**

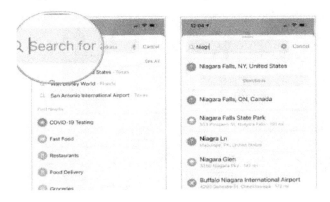

- Navigate down and tap the **share sheet icon**

- Next, send via your **preferred medium**

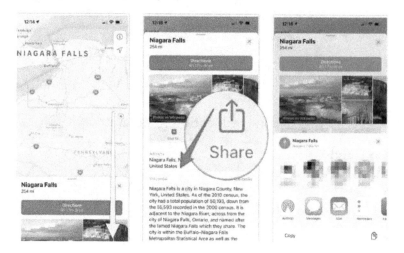

Getting Directions with Siri and Maps

- Activate Siri by saying **"Hey Siri"**

- You can say something like: **"directions to the white house"**

- Next, choose a **mode of transportation.**

- Click **Go** to begin navigation immediately.

Using Siri and Maps to Locate Local Businesses

- Activate Siri by saying **"Hey Siri"**

- Next, let siri know what you want by saying something like: "directions to the nearest bank"

- Select **your preferred option** in case siri presents more than one

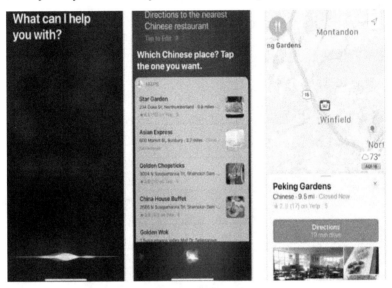

- Click a **mode of transportation** or siri will revert to Drive or Walk based on how close you are to the destination

- Click **Go** to begin the navigation or Siri would start running in a few seconds

Finding Your Way Home via Siri and Maps

- Activate siri by saying **"Hey Siri"**

- Say: **"take me home"**

- Select a **mode of transportation**

- Click **Start** to begin the navigation or it will automatically do so within a few seconds

To also enable location services:

- Go to **Settings**

- Go to **Privacy**

- Go to **Location Services**

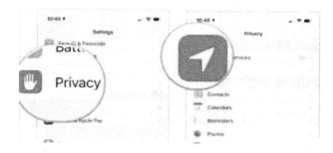

- Click **Maps**

- Select **While Using The App** from Allow Location Access

You also need to engage Significant Locations. Follow these steps:

- Go to **Settings**

- Go to **Privacy**

- Go to **Location Services**

- Navigate down and tap **System Services**

- Switch On **Significant Locations**

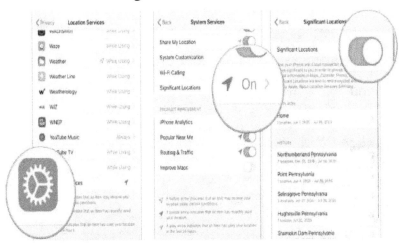

Changing the Navigation Voice Volume

- Go to **Settings**

- Click on **Maps**

- Click **Navigation & Guidance**

- Choose the **desired volume level**

Deleting Recent Destination and Search History

- Go to **Maps**

- Swipe **up** to see the **recents** menu

- Swipe to the **left** on a set of directions or a place to call up the **More** menu

- Click **Delete**

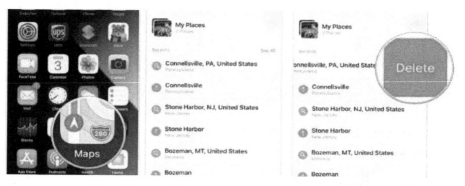

Viewing the Weather in Maps

- Open **Maps**

- Push the **weather button** at lower right corner. There may be a need for you to **zoom in** on the map to make the weather button show up

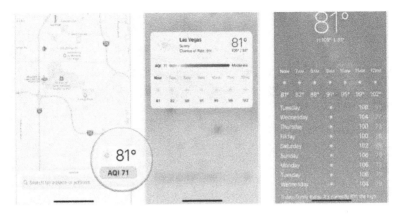

Opening Apple Maps Locations in Google Maps

- Download opener

- Go to **Apple maps**

- Next, **Search** for a location

- **Swipe up** on the information screen to reveal the share button

- **Click** the **share button**

- Select **opener**

- Choose the option **Open Link in Google Maps**

- Click **Open** to affirm that you want to run the directions in Google Maps and Select **Start** in Google Maps to start the journey

Chapter 18: Apple Arcade

The arcade is a new gaming subscription service that's available in the App store and compatible with all Apple devices running iOS 13. You get access to over a hundred premium games with new ones added every week. The best thing of all is that there's something for everyone and it costs just $5 a month.

Signing Up

- Open the **App** store

- Click on **Arcade** at bottom menu bar

- Click **Try It Free** to begin a one-month free trial. After the trial period, you can now start paying the monthly fee of $4.99 or yearly fee of $49.99

- Click **confirm** to begin the trial and sign up for Apple Arcade

Canceling Apple Arcade

- Go to the **App Store**

- Click on your **Apple ID** at top right

- Choose **Subscriptions**

- Choose **Apple Arcade**

- Click **Cancel Free Trial** or **Cancel Subscription**

Using Family Sharing with Apple Arcade

Apple included the ability to share with five family members and it's all at that same price. This means that you should have family sharing set up and running. In case you haven't, here's how:

Getting Started with Family Sharing

A family member, who would be the family organizer should set it up. Such a person must have the capability to foot the bill for purchases made by members of the group

- Open **Settings**
- Click on the **Apple ID banner** at the top
- Click on **Set Up Family Sharing**

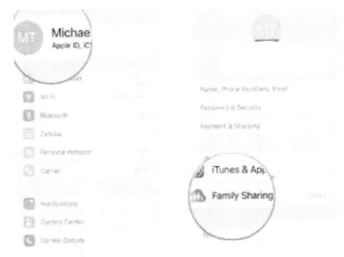

- Click on **Get started**
- Click on **Continue**
- Click again on **Continue** to share purchases

- Click **Continue** to confirm your method of payment

- Click **Share Your Location** to share it with Family members or you can click **Not Now**

- Click **Add Family Member**

- Enter someone's **name**

- Click the **Person** you want to add as a family member

- Key in the **credit card security code** when asked to so as to affirm you are the family organizer

- You can keep adding members until the numbers are complete.

Accepting a Family Sharing Invitation

- Open **Settings**

- Click on the **Apple ID banner** at the top

- Click **Invitations**

- Click **Accept**

Click **confirm**

Click **continue** to share purchases

Click to **Share your location** or tap **Not Now**

Selecting and Playing a Game

- Open the **App Store**

- Access the **Arcade** section

- Search through and find a **game** that you want to play

- Click the **Get** button when viewing a game to start the download

- When the **downloading** is done, click on play

- You can also play any Apple Arcade game by tapping the icon from your **Home screen** to open it

Playing a Game on a Different Device

- Open **Settings**

- Click on your **Apple ID** at top

- Click **iCloud**

- Choose **Manage Storage**

- Navigate down and locate the **game** you want to **manage save data** for

- Click the **game** to access it

- You can also tap **Delete** data to erase it

In case of issues with Apple Arcade, you may want to take the following steps:

- Signing out of your Apple ID and signing back in if you are having downloading issues

- You can reboot or reset your device

- In the case of family sharing, ensure that you have it properly set up

Chapter 19: Podcasts

With Apple podcasts, you can stream and download all your favorite shows and even discover new ones while at it. That's not all. You can still subscribe, sync and customize podcasts to your desire.

Finding, subscribing to and Streaming/downloading Podcasts

- Launch **podcasts**

- Click **Search** in the menu at screen bottom

- Enter the **name** or **genre** of podcast you seek

- Click **Search** at bottom right

- When you find what you seek, **tap** on it

- Click **Subscribe**

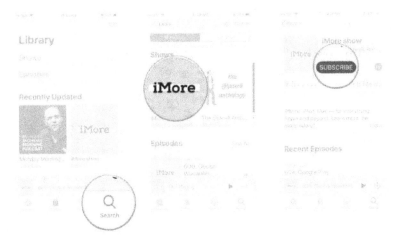

- Click the **download** button next to the episode name.

- Click the **episode** you want to listen to stream it without downloading

Sharing Podcasts and Podcast Episodes

- Open **podcasts**

- Click the **podcast** or click **Details** on the **episode** you want to share. Click the **more** button

- Click **share**

- Click the **method** you want to use to share the podcast or episode. Share normally

Syncing Podcasts Across Devices

- Go to **Settings.** Click **Podcasts**

- Click the **button** next to **sync Podcasts**

Setting the Refresh Rate for Podcasts

- Go to **Settings.** Click **Podcasts**

- Click **Refresh Every**

- Click **how often** you would want your podcasts to update.
  Choose between **1 hour, 6 hours, Day, Week, Manually**

Turning off Delete Played Episodes for Podcasts

- Open **Settings**

- Click **Podcasts**

- Click the **button** next to **Delete Played Episodes** to turn it off

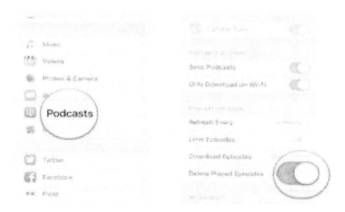

Turning off Notifications for Podcasts

- Open **Settings**

- Click **Podcasts**

- Click **Notifications**

Chapter 20: Find My

This is a feature that combines the functions of Find my iPhone and Find my friends in one app. It's available for iOS 13. Via this app you can share your location with friends and family, view friend locations that has been shared with you. It's also possible for you to track down, remotely lock and wipe lost devices.

Finding Friends in Find My

- Launch **Find My**
- Click on the **People** tab if the app doesn't open to it
- Click the **friend** sharing their location in the list below the map

- Next, swipe upwards on the card and click **Contact** to view that friend's contact information
- Click **Directions** to directed to their location in Maps
- Click **Add (Friend's name) to Favorites**

- Click **Edit Location name**

- Click a **label** to the location for e.g. Home, gym, school etc.

- Click **Add Custom Label** to create a custom label for their location

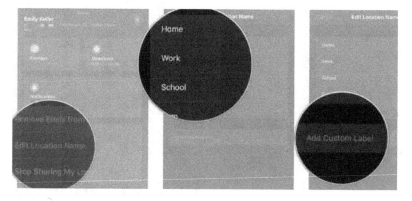

Sharing your Location

- Launch **Find My**

- Click on the **Me** tab

- Click the button next to **Share My Location**

Notifying Friends of Your Location

- Launch **Find My**

- Click the **People** tab in case the app doesn't open to it

- Click a **friend** who is sharing their location in the list below the map

- Swipe upwards and click **Add...** under **Notifications**

- Click **Notify (friend's name)**

- Choose between **When I arrive** or **When I Leave** depending on the preference

- Click on the **location** the notification will be about

- You can also click **Add Location** to add a new location then the listed one

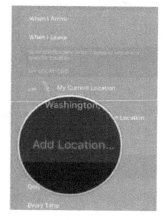

- Choose between **Only Once** or **Every Time** depending on the preference

- Click **Add**

Marking a Device as Lost

- Launch **Find My**

- Click the **Devices** tab and the nearby devices should appear

- Click the device you want to locate

- Swipe upwards and click **Activate** under **Mark as Lost**

- Click **Continue**

- You can choose to **enter your phone number**

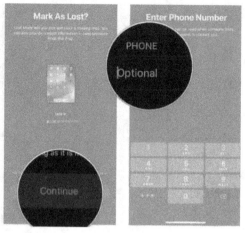

- Click **Next**

- You can **leave a message** for the finder of your device

- Click **Activate**

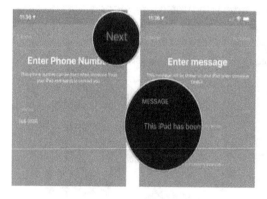

Erasing a Device Remotely

- Launch **Find My**

- Click the **Devices** tab and the nearby ones will show up on the map

- Click the device you want to erase

- Swipe up and click on **Erase This Device**

- Click **Erase This Device**

- You can decide to **enter your phone number**

- Click **Next**

- You can decide to **leave a message** for a finder

- Click **Erase**

Managing Your Personal Settings in Find My

- Launch **Find My**

- Click on **Me**

- Swipe up and click the switch close to **Share My Location** to start or stop the sharing of your location

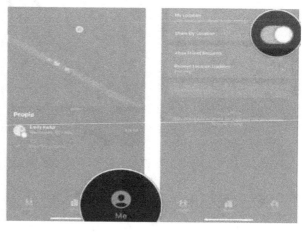

- Click the **switch** next to **Allow Friend Requests**

- Click **Receive Location Updates** to decide who receives updates on your position

- Choose between **people you share with** or **Everyone**

- **Click** Me

- Click **Edit Location Name**

- Click a **label** e.g school, Home, work etc

- click **Add Custom Label** to choose a new custom label for their location

Chapter 21: Face Time

Every apple product has a built in Face Time app. You have the option of doing audio or video calls over a Wi-Fi or cellular data connection. You can stay in touch with family, friends and colleagues even while on the move or traveling. It's very easy to use.

Making a Face Time Audio or Video Call

- Launch **Face Time** on your device

- Click the **+** symbol

- Enter the **name, email address** or **number** you want to call

- In case you want to do a group call, you can type more **names, Addresses** or **numbers**

- Click **Audio** or **Video** to begin the call

Switching from a Normal Call to Face Time

- View the **call menu** that shows when you are on a call

- Next, click the Face Time button to begin a Face Time video call

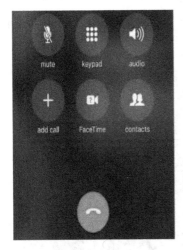 

Turning off Video from a Face Time Call

- **Initiate** or **take** a Face Time call

- Push the **Home Button** or **swipe up** from screen bottom depending on your device and the video feed will be put on hold but the other party would still hear you

Using Siri to Place a Face Time Call

- Push and hold the **Home button** or the **Side button** or say "**Hey Siri**" to engage the voice assistant

- Say **"Face Time + (name)** or say **"Face Time"** and wait for Siri's prompt before speaking the name of the person you want to call. Siri would now initiate the call

Using Face Time with Apple TV

- **Swipe upwards** from screen bottom or swipe down on right corner of Home screen depending on device

- Click **Screen Mirroring**

- Click on the device to which you want to mirror your device's screen

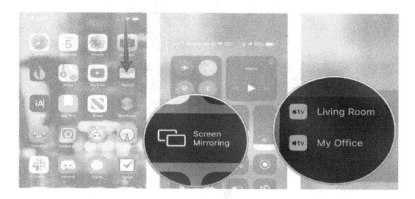

Chapter 22: Trouble Shooting

Sometimes, your device can start acting up and leaves you a bit stranded when you need it the most. Sometimes it could be minor hiccups which can be sorted out by some trouble shooting procedure and sometimes, you just can't avoid taking it for professional handling—usually after all else has failed. So here are the steps you can take to handle things on your end and if it doesn't sort the issue, then escalate to qualified service personnel.

Powering off or Restarting Your Device

Sometimes you might experience some slowing down and malfunctioning of your device that a simple powering off and restart would solve.

- Press and hold down the **on/Off** button on the right side or top depending on your device for about 3 seconds

- Move the **Slide to Power off** confirmation slider to the right

Doing a Forced Reset

- First, click and let go of the **Volume Up** button

- Secondly, click and let go of the **Volume down** button

- Next press and hold onto the sleep/wake on/off **side** button

- Hold the **side** button even after the shutdown screen shows up

Putting your Device into Recovery Mode

- Make sure that iTunes is closed on your computer

- **Plug** your USB to Lightning cable into your **computer**

- Next, **plug** the USB to Lightning cable to your **phone**

- Run **iTunes**

- Press and let go of the **Volume Up button** and **Volume Down button**

- Press and hold the **Side** button till you see the recovery mode screen

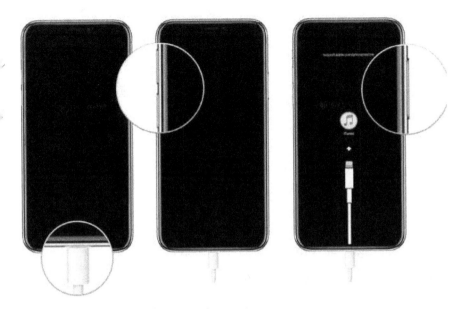

Resetting all of Your Device's settings

- Open the **Settings app.** Click **General.** Click **Reset**

- Click **Reset All Settings**

Resetting Your Network Settings

- Open **Settings.** Click **General.** Click **Reset**

- Click **Reset Network Settings.** Enter your passcode if need be

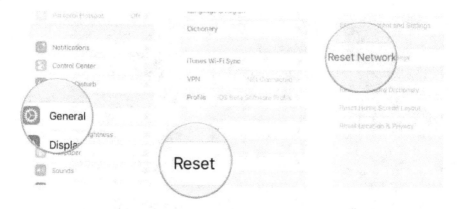

Resetting your keyboard Dictionary

- Open **Settings.** Click **General.** Click **Reset**

- Click **Reset Keyboard Dictionary**. Enter your passcode if asked

Resetting Home Screen Layout

- Open **Settings. Click General.** Click **Reset**

- Click **Reset Home Screen Layout.** Enter your passcode if prompted

Resetting Location and Privacy

- Open **Settings.** Click **General.** Click **Reset**

- Click **Reset Location & Privacy.** Enter your passcode if prompted

Erasing and Restoring your Device to Factory Settings

- Open **Settings.** Click **General.** Click **Reset**

- Click **Erase All Content and Settings**

Phone not charging?

Try the following:

- Force a restart using the steps outlined in **How do to a forced Reset** above

- Try a different port or outlet

- Switch or change cables

- Restore using iTunes

- If all else fails, contact Apple

Battery Life Unusual?

If you are sure that your battery performance is less than stellar, and you have made sure that there are no apps consuming too much power and you have equally checked the battery health to confirm that there is indeed a problem, try the following:

- Do a **reset** following steps as outlined above
- **Restore as new** by erasing all content and return to factory settings and set up as new (follow steps in erasing and restoring device to factory settings)

Turning on Low Power Mode

- Open **Settings**
- Click **Battery**
- Turn on **Low Power Mode**

If all steps do not rectify the situation, it's time to go see an Apple Authorized service provider.

Phone Not Powering On?

- Make sure the battery is fully charged. Connect to a power source and try again

- Try a **hard reset**

Doing a Restore Using iTunes Via Mac or Window PC

- Connect your device to iTunes on Mac or PC using Lightning or 30 pin dock connector

- Click on **Device** tab at top left

- Click **Backup**

- Let the backup finish

- click on **Restore**

- Allow it to finish

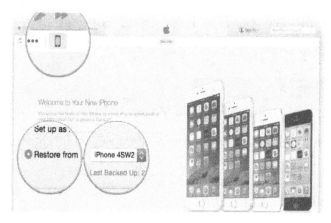

If all fails, contact Apple.